"*The Crystal Alchemist* offers the wisdom and guidance you need to get started with the world of crystals. It provides empowering information to further your crystal journey and experience the transformative energy of crystals."

> —**Heather Askinosie**, founder of Energy Muse, author of
> CRYSTAL365, and coauthor of *Crystal Muse*

"*The Crystal Alchemist* is a powerhouse of knowledge, revealing fascinating facts in every chapter, and including everything you need to know to start or enhance your crystal collection. Karen Frazier shares a wealth of expertise from the basics, such as how to choose the right crystals to the intricate structure and the healing properties of your precious collection. This book is perfect for anyone who loves crystals or is drawn to their beauty and spiritual vibration."

> —**Karen A. Anderson**, award-winning afterlife expert and
> animal communicator, and best-selling and award-winning author
> of *The Amazing Afterlife of Animals* and *Hear All Creatures!*

"Karen Frazier has created a beautiful guide to the understanding and use of crystals. She gives us the science as well as the art of what crystals do and how to use them. Her work is engaging and comes not just from study, but from her own experience as well. When I have a client needing assistance with crystals, Karen is the only one I refer them to."

> —**William Becker, MPA**, board member of various historical
> organizations, educator, author, and psychic medium

"*The Crystal Alchemist* by Karen Frazier is a must-read. It is full of wonderful information from a scientific approach, as well as from a metaphysical perspective. I especially love how Karen explains that crystals are a form of consciousness that one communicates with on an energetic level. If you want to learn a fun and simple way to understand crystals from color to shape and everything in between, then *The Crystal Alchemist* will be a great addition to your books on crystals."

—**Sharon Lewis "AurorA"**, psychic medium; author; and energy
healer using various modalities, including crystals

"This book contains everything you need to know about crystals from A to Z. Whether you're just starting out or have years of experience working with crystals, this book is for you. Karen not only shares her personal experiences working with crystals but teaches you many different applications on how to use them in your own daily life."

—**Kristen Gray**, case manager at White Light Paranormal Insight,
and coordinator with the Oregon Ghost Conference

"Crystals are alive with the vibration of the universe, energetically interacting with their environment. *The Crystal Alchemist* teaches practical ways to choose, harness, direct, and amplify the inherent healing properties of the mineral kingdom. Author Karen Frazier not only sheds light on the sacred principles of crystals for personal transformation, she provides a road map for living in conscious relationship with their energetic frequency. Full of grounded examples, it's an inspirational book of personal empowerment not only found from crystal work, but discovered within oneself, as the recipes for change are applied and become crystal clear."

—**Karen A. Dahlman, MA**, licensed professional counselor,
talk show host, and author of *The Spirit of Alchemy*

"From the age of innocence, Karen Frazier instinctively knew about and fell in love with the transformative abilities, sentient qualities, and vibrating energy fields present in the many rocks and crystals she came to adore as a child. This same soulful intrigue has carried over to her adult years where she has spent countless hours studying metaphysics and the multitude of benefits of utilizing rocks and crystals. With a gifted style for written prose and impeccable credentials as a metaphysical practitioner, let Karen Frazier be your mentor as you learn about the many positive ways crystals can integrate into your life."

—**Nicole Strickland, BA, MS**, former educator and school counselor, published author, and writer for *Paranormal Underground* magazine

"With images allowing you to almost feel the power, you will gain a resource and a clear understanding in this beautiful and approachable guide written by an author who has a passion and enthusiasm for the world of crystals."

—**Patrick Keller**, educator, blogger, and host of the *Big Seance Podcast*

"*The Crystal Alchemist* is a fascinating guide that outlines the wonderful world of crystals and how to use them to positively transform your everyday life. Karen Frazier's comprehensive yet easy-to-read guidebook details gems and stones of all types, and how you can unlock the ultimate power within them. As an expert in both the metaphysical and physical realms, Karen shares valuable insights about how to choose the right crystals for you, how to effectively use 'these ancient gifts from the planet,' and how to take care of your crystals to maximize their true power."

—**Cheryl Knight**, editor in chief *of Paranormal Underground* magazine

THE
CRYSTAL
ALCHEMIST

A COMPREHENSIVE GUIDE *to*
UNLOCKING *the* TRANSFORMATIVE POWER
of GEMS & STONES

KAREN FRAZIER

REVEAL PRESS
AN IMPRINT OF NEW HARBINGER PUBLICATIONS

Publisher's Note

Distributed in Canada by Raincoast Books

Copyright © 2019 by Karen Frazier
          Reveal Press
          An imprint of New Harbinger Publications, Inc.
          5674 Shattuck Avenue
          Oakland, CA 94609
          www.newharbinger.com

Cover design by Sara Christian

Interior design by Michele Waters-Kermes

Interior photos licensed through Shutterstock

Acquired by Ryan Buresh

Edited by Gretel Hakanson

Library of Congress Cataloging-in-Publication Data on file

Printed in China

21

10   9   8   7   6   5   4   3   2

Contents

PART 4: The Crystal Habit

iv

Crystals in Everyday Life

For as long as I can remember, crystals and stones have been a significant part of my life. As a child, I collected rocks. I grew up in coastal Washington State, where I spent hours on rocky beaches sifting through stones to find the perfect addition to my collection.

While I was always on the lookout for shiny agates, no stone was so insignificant it escaped my intense interest. I dug in flower beds, sifted through gravel in parking lots, scanned riverbeds and mountain trails, and dug through any pile of stones I could find to gather rocks that met my fancy.

I kept a box in the basement to house my growing collection, and I frequently visited it to sort through my treasures, holding and loving each as a piece of beauty from the Earth. Regardless of what the rocks looked like, holding them made me feel good, although I lacked the frame of reference at the time to understand why this might be. My time spent with my rocks left me feeling both peaceful and energized.

Even then, I instinctively understood what has come to be my guiding philosophy regarding rocks, minerals, gems, and crystals. Stones are gifts from the planet. Each, regardless of how it looks on the outside, houses great beauty.

I believe crystals and stones are beings that vibrate with ancient energy. When we live and work with them, their energy can't help but affect ours. At their most basic structure, crystals are made of the same material as we are. They are comprised of vibrating strands of energy held together by fields to form matter. It's the same way all matter in our universe—including rocks, trees, plants, and people—is formed from pure energy into conscious entities. The consciousness of the universe permeates all matter—not just sentient beings. However, because the energy that makes up inanimate objects forms into structures that appear nonsentient, we must communicate with them energetically instead of how we've come to communicate with things we perceive as "alive," such as plants, animals, and people. Therefore, communication and communion with crystals and other sacred objects occurs energetically instead of intellectually. Through consciousness activities such as meditation, intention, and ritual, as well as by sharing our space with crystals, we can combine their vibration with ours to create something that is greater than the sum of its parts. Crystals can enhance our lives with their ancient energy if we allow them to do so.

My collection of stones, so enthusiastically gathered, moldered in my parents' basement when I went off to college and later moved into a series of small apartments and homes where I didn't have room for much. When my parents sold my childhood home, I imagine they found my box of rocks and returned my childhood friends to the wild for someone else to find and love.

As young adulthood took over, I mostly forgot about my collection, although my love for rocks never fully disappeared. When I saw them in shops, I was always drawn to the crystals, but different financial priorities took precedent, and other than a shiny bauble here and there, I didn't have many crystals and stones.

It wasn't until my thirties that I was reminded of my interest in stones and I began, once again, to invite their energy into my life. It started with a sore throat. It was a bad one, and it lasted for days and then weeks without lessening despite medical intervention. Finally, in desperation, I decided to try a different type of a treatment, and I located a medical doctor who was also an energy healer and Reiki practitioner. While I'd always had an interest in Reiki and energy healing, I'd never tried it because even though I thought it sounded cool, it also seemed pretty out there and something a responsible adult wouldn't spend limited funds on. But I was desperate, which provided me with an excuse to try something I'd always wanted to experience. Plus, since the practitioner was a medical doctor, I thought it possible my insurance might cover any alternative treatments I received.

At my appointment, the doctor had me lie on a treatment table where she placed crystals on various points on my body and did energy work with her hands. My analytical mind told me how stupid the whole thing was, and I kept trying to ask her about how this all worked *medically* and *scientifically*. She politely told me to relax and allow. I didn't.

However, in spite of my whirling mind, attempts at logical thought, and unwillingness to allow, something happened. I felt a huge release and started crying. I rode a wave of emotion, crying on and off for three days. And my sore throat went away. I'd never experienced anything like that before, nor had I ever had such a sudden cessation of persistent symptoms. It was the first time I truly understood the connection between body, mind, and spirit and how all three were so interconnected it was impossible to separate them and treat only one. It also opened my mind to the possibility that energetic modalities of healing, like using crystals, could address this connection by vibrationally affecting the energy that made up me. My skepticism softened, and as I began to explore crystals and other energy healing modalities, it eventually faded.

That was the start of my journey into understanding the human energy field. That single experience led to my intense study of metaphysics and energy healing, my education and work as a Reiki master, my pursuit of advanced degrees in metaphysical science (I'm currently pursuing a doctorate of divinity in spiritual healing and hold a master's in metaphysical science and a PhD in metaphysical parapsychology), and it was the genesis of my fascination with all types of energy healing modalities, including crystals, sound healing, and various other forms of vibrational work. I've written two books about crystals (*Crystals for Healing* and *Crystals for Beginners*), a book about Reiki (*Reiki Healing for Beginners*), and a book about empowering your life through energy healing (*The Higher Vibes Toolbox*). I teach classes in crystals, Reiki, fêng shui and space energetics, sound healing, and energy healing in Portland, Oregon.

Perhaps not surprisingly, my home and life are filled with crystals. In fact, it turns out my love of rocks may be a genetic trait. After my dad's recent death, I discovered in his office several rocks he'd kept and placed around his space. And in cleaning my son's room after he left for college, I discovered his stash of rocks, tucked away on a windowsill beside his bed.

The love of crystals, it seems, is a multigenerational trait in my family passed down from father to daughter to son.

Examples of Crystals in Action

I use crystals in every aspect of my life, and I often use them in my other practices as well.

I have a friend who owns a boutique hotel. A few years ago, a flash flood filled her basement with mud and debris, destroying everything she had stored there. Damage was in the tens of thousands of dollars. My friend was, naturally, affected by the flooding. A group of us headed to the hotel and spent a day mucking out the basement shortly after the flood.

I'd spent many hours in the basement prior to the flood, and while we were mucking, I noticed how flat the energy felt. It felt heavy and uncomfortable, and my friend agreed. A few weeks later, the same group returned to the basement to cleanse it in a different way. We burned sacred herbs (sage and palo santo), and I scattered various crystals throughout the basement. I placed smoky quartz around the perimeter to transmute the negative energy from the flood into positive energy. I added clear quartz to magnify the positive energy. I placed citrine in strategic spots to promote success, prosperity, and abundance. I also placed black tourmaline to absorb any remaining negative energy. After doing so, we noticed an immediate change in the energy of the basement, and my friend and the hotel have moved in a positive direction since.

In another example, I was called to help a family who was struggling to sell their home. The property had been on the market for several years, and every time the sellers were close to a sale, it fell through during escrow. This happened several times.

When I visited the house, the family hadn't lived there for years. As I walked the very large property (about 10 acres) with multiple outbuildings, I felt heaviness. The energy of the place felt negative, and it left me feeling stressed, angry, and worn out. If I'd been a potential buyer, I suspect I would have passed regardless of the property's many charms.

After consultation with the owner, I discovered that while it was a beloved and happy family home for years, later life events brought negativity. One of the family members was accused of murder in their later years in the home, and the family slowly fell apart. Likewise, one of the family members worked as a hospice nurse and provided end-of-life care for many people who died on the property.

Crystals were my main focus of energy work for the property. I first scattered black tourmaline to absorb the negativity from the past and rimmed the property with smoky quartz to help transmute negative energy to positive. Then, I worked in various locations with the energy by adding different crystals to create energetic balance where imbalance existed. Finally, I scattered rose quartz to promote unconditional love and attraction and citrine for success. Within a few weeks, the house sold after languishing for nearly a decade on the market, and a new family is building loving energy there now.

Crystals also work with human energy in a similar way. Recently, a close friend lost his mother. He lived with her and cared for her his entire adult life, and they were extremely close. At the funeral, I gave him a piece of Apache tears, which is a form of obsidian known for helping with and transmuting grief. My friend later shared with me that he always keeps the crystal with him and he feels it is helping him be in a place of peace with his mom's passing.

Likewise, I recently had a deeply personal experience with crystals. My father died a few months ago after a short and painful battle with stage 4 lung cancer. My family was with him in hospice in his last days of life. While we spent most of our time at his side, occasionally one of us would leave for an hour or so. When it was my turn to take a break, my husband and I went to a local crystal shop. I was seeking something to help me process the stress, grief, and sadness I was experiencing at the imminent loss of my father and focusing mostly on how various pieces felt to me energetically. I was drawn to a necklace made from a blue crystal (Siberian blue quartz, it turned out) cut in a diamond shape with a smaller round white crystal (danburite) attached to the top. It was expensive, but I was drawn to it and purchased it. We returned to my dad's hospice room with me wearing the new necklace.

Shortly after our return, my father took a turn, and it was clear he had entered the final few hours or moments of his life. As we stood beside him, I felt a shift in the energy of the room. I felt as if others had entered the room (although there was no one there I could physically see), and I turned to my husband and quietly signaled that dad's loved ones in spirit had come for him and this would be his last breath. It was. I felt him leave with those who had come to escort him to the other side.

As we traveled back to our hotel a few hours later, wrung out, grieving, and exhausted, I kept hearing my dad's voice. I suspected it was my imagination, but I didn't want it to be. When we got to the hotel room, my husband stepped out for a moment, and I heard my dad's voice say clearly, "Hey! Listen to me!" I felt someone physically tug on my hair. And so, I allowed that conversation with my dad, imagination or not.

Later, I looked up the necklace I'd purchased, curious about what its purported metaphysical properties were based on the crystals and the specific cut (it was made by an artisan who cuts specific crystals into sacred geometric shapes to enhance certain properties). It turns out the crystal necklace I'd purchased on instinct was designed to enhance communication with higher realms, the Divine, and people who have passed away.

Experiencing Crystals for Yourself

I am a true believer in how these ancient gifts from the planet can affect the energy aspects of life, from my own personal vibration to the energy of the spaces in which I live, play, and work. Crystals are part of every moment of every day for me in one way or another, whether I'm wearing them, sitting near them, teaching or writing about them, or working with them specifically.

I make no secret of the fact that I started out as a huge skeptic, so I understand the skepticism of others well. Even now at times I find myself thinking, *There's no way this can work*, but experience repeatedly shows me otherwise. I have had far more success in my life turning to energetic and crystal solutions for issues of health, well-being, emotions, relationships, prosperity, and many others than I ever have to conventional solutions. When I feel stuck, I use crystals and other energetic modalities, and I'm always filled with wonder at how quickly and effectively they help unstick me and get me moving in a positive direction once again.

Of course, I can share multiple personal anecdotes, but any number of my positive experiences won't be as effective as you having a single experience of your own. Which is why I offer you a simple suggestion: try it. Start with something small, find the right crystal, approach it with an open mind, allow for change, and see how it works for you. I believe you will be as amazed as I was by how crystals can help bring desired energies into your life if you allow them to do so.

The Elegant Simplicity of Crystals

I use crystals because I love them, because I believe they improve my energy and the energy in my environment, and because they are beautiful. Crystals make me feel good, and they always have.

I also recommend them for another reason. Crystals are simple. You don't need to have much knowledge to work with them. You can bring a crystal into your environment, and without doing another single thing, the crystal will affect the energy in that environment. Crystals affect vibration with minimal effort. You don't need to know any other energy healing principles, and you don't need to be attuned to energy healing techniques. If a certain crystal calls to you or interests you, chances are you need the energy that crystal offers in your life. Crystals are efficient, mostly affordable, widely available, and incredibly user-friendly.

Your Crystal Journey

In the chapters that follow, I offer you the tools you need to begin to bring the ancient energy of crystals into your life. It isn't necessary to be steeped in crystals for them to have positive effects. I provide you with a system for understanding which types of crystals—based on color, type, and lattice structure—will support the energy you desire in your life. Then I provide you with tools for selecting them, cleansing and programming them, using them in your home and workspace, wearing them, using them with intention, creating crystal combinations that support specific goals, and using them to attract energies into your life via intention, affirmation, meditation, and visualization processes. Finally, I cover the basics to turn working with crystal energy into a habit that supports you and combining it with other energy healing practices to bring even more harmonious energy into your life.

You can choose to use as few or as many of these tools as you wish. Choose any of the tools that resonate with you so you can live with crystals in a way that brings you joy, peace, and balance.

I am excited and honored you have allowed me to help you embark on this sacred journey in your life.

PART 1

THE BASICS
OF CRYSTALS

CHAPTER 1

What Are Crystals, and How Do They Work?

My goal is to help you discover a way to understand crystal properties without needing to look them up in a printed or online resource. To do this, I will help you understand why certain crystals vibrate in tune with specific energies based on the lattice system of the crystal, its color, and its opacity. Understanding these three qualities and how they affect the crystals' healing properties will provide you with plenty of information to go confidently into a crystal shop to find a gemstone that will suit your purposes.

After reading this, you will be able to decide which crystals you want without the need for further references. Even so, printed and online crystal resources are valuable, and contain excellent information about the various specific properties of healing crystals. If you wish to deepen your practice and understanding, you can use these resources either independently or in conjunction with the information you'll find in this book. I own multiple crystal references (and I've written a few myself), and I consult them from time to time when I'm seeking something specific. I also use the references to identify crystals I find or own but can't remember what they are. Given the sheer number of crystals I own, this happens more often than you might imagine.

What Are Crystals?

Many people use the term "crystal" for any type of rock they gather that has healing properties, but geologically, there are terms that mean specific things. In the context of this book, I'll use the terms "crystals" and "gemstones" in the common fashion, which is to mean any rock with vibrational healing properties, but I want to offer you the geological definitions of each term, as well.

MINERALS

Minerals are naturally occurring inorganic (doesn't contain living tissue) substances that are solid. They contain one or more elements (such as calcium and carbon) and have a specific chemical composition. Minerals also have a specific crystalline structure. Therefore, all minerals are crystals. However, there are some substances (such as mercury) that are solid substances with a specific chemical composition that don't have a crystalline structure. These are mineraloids, and not minerals. All minerals are rocks, but not all rocks are specific minerals.

Some examples of minerals include calcite, which is calcium carbonate; fluorite, which is calcium fluorite; and quartz, which is silicon dioxide.

ROCKS

Rocks, also called stones, are naturally occurring materials made up of two or more minerals. An example of this is granite, which contains quartz, feldspar, and small amounts of other minerals like mica. So in the case of

your granite countertop, it is a rock that contains a combination of various crystalline minerals including quartz. Fossils are rocks that contain various minerals. So is limestone, which is 50 percent calcite and 50 percent other substances, as is the substance known as septarian, which is a combination of aragonite, calcite, and limestone. All rocks contain minerals.

CRYSTALS

Crystals are minerals. They are an inorganic material comprised of a specific chemical composition with an internal lattice pattern that occurs in various shapes. There are six specific lattice patterns in crystals that determine the crystal's type. I will discuss these later. All crystals are rocks, but not all rocks are crystals.

GEMSTONES

Gemstones, or gems, are precious and semiprecious minerals that have a specific color and clarity. Gemstones are assigned monetary value based on characteristics such as durability, rarity, color, cut, and clarity. Examples of precious gemstones include diamonds, rubies, and sapphires, while semiprecious gemstone examples include citrine, clear quartz, and amethyst.

These are the definitions of crystals that geologists use in classifying rocks and stones in a scientific manner. However, in the language of healing crystals, you will often see other substances with vibrational healing properties referred to as crystals when they don't meet the specific, scientific definition of the term. For example, Baltic amber is petrified tree sap found in the region of the Baltic Sea, but you'll find it listed as a healing crystal in most resources despite the fact that it doesn't meet the scientific definition of a crystal, mineral, or rock. The same is true of petrified wood (it doesn't meet the inorganic criteria because it was once living) and of man-made substances now referred to as crystals, such as orgonite (or orgone), goldstone, and bronzite. Likewise, you'll find some rocks, like lapis lazuli (a combination of pyrite, lazurite, calcite, and sodalite), called crystals when they don't meet the technical and scientific definitions of such.

While you are now aware of the various definitions, in this book, I will sometimes refer to other substances that aren't technically crystals as crystals due to their uses and healing properties. I will use the metaphysical definition of crystals as opposed to the scientific classification.

How Do Crystals Work?

Crystals get their power from the same source as everything else in this universe. Everything is made up of energy. Quantum theory shows when you examine the tiniest levels of matter, it is all vibrating strands of energy surrounded by vast empty spaces. Energetic fields hold these vibrating strands in shapes that make up the matter we see in the universe and experience as solid material. Every physical aspect of you, every bodily function, every thought you think, and every emotion you have are all made up of energy.

The scientific principle known as the "conservation of energy" shows how, in a closed system, energy can neither be created nor destroyed. It can only convert from one form to another. An example of this is water. Water, which exists as a form of potential energy, falls from the sky and flows into lakes, rivers, oceans, streams, and groundwater, where it becomes kinetic energy (energy in motion). All of these bodies of water have the capacity to operate turbines (mechanical energy) that generate the electrical energy that powers our world. In this way, the potential energy of water becomes kinetic energy, mechanical energy, and then electrical energy.

Einstein demonstrated with his special theory of relativity that mass can become energy and energy can become mass ($E = mc^2$); mass is one form energy takes. Quantum theory takes Einstein's work further, showing the underlying vibrational nature of all matter in the universe and leading to an understanding that what appears solid is merely the perception of vibrational energy held together by fields to form what seems to be solid objects. Energy underpins the structure of our physical universe. Everything is oscillation. Everything is vibration.

Spiritual views of the underlying energy of everything in the universe reach the same conclusions as science; they just approach it from a different angle. Many metaphysical and energy healing scholars have written about these concepts, such as author Lynne McTaggart in her work *The Field*, in which she explains how quantum views of energy line up with spiritual and metaphysical beliefs about the connectedness of all animate and inanimate matter via a soup of entangled quantum vibration she calls "the field." Similarly, the Buddhist principle of *Dzogchen* (the Great Perfection) holds that all physical, mental, and emotional phenomena are expressions of energy that exist in the consciousness of infinite space. In other words, everything is energy, including you, your thoughts, your consciousness, and your very being.

Just as you are made up of vibrating energy, so are crystals. Their energy exists in structured patterns known geologically as "lattice systems" that have specific internal geometric shapes. These lattice systems hold an electric charge called "piezoelectricity." When subjected to mechanical stress (such as pressure), objects with piezoelectricity release an electrical charge. Because of this effect, some crystals are used in electronics, such as the quartz in watches.

Because both crystals and you have an energetic frequency, when you come into contact with a crystal, the vibration of one affects the frequency of the other. This occurs through a process called "entrainment," a principle discovered by Dutch scientist Christiaan Huygens in 1665. He noticed that two pendulum clocks hung side by side on the same wall gradually move into synchronicity, so the pendulums, while originally swinging at different rates, lock into phase and begin to swing together. This phenomena, also known as "mode locking," is repeatable and has been shown in multiple experiments, such as those used with mechanical metronomes and other pendulum clocks. Just as clocks and metronomes lock into phase, various energies entrain in energy healing and crystal use. When we bring a crystal into an environment or work with it physically, the energetics of that environment or person entrain with the energy of the crystals.

Powerful Agents of Change

While crystals may seem like inanimate objects, they aren't. Each crystal vibrates and is connected to the energetic field that flows throughout the universe, affecting the frequency of everything. Each crystal has specific properties that determine its frequency and how it affects the vibration of all other energetic structures. With a basic understanding of these principles, you can use crystals as powerful tools to create intentional change in your life, health, well-being, spirituality, and environment.

CHAPTER 2

Colors and Opacity

The colors of crystals as well as their opacity, or transparency, affect their vibration. The main thing I teach in my classes is this: if you can't remember anything else, simply remember the properties of crystal colors and opacity, and you'll likely be able to choose a crystal for the situation you are trying to heal.

Color

Color occurs as the result of how the eye perceives light, which is a vibrational frequency. It was Isaac Newton who originally described the visible spectrum of light as electromagnetic frequency visible to the human eye. We perceive differences in this spectrum as color. Therefore, color, like everything else, has a vibrational frequency and a wavelength, so it is merely another manifestation of energy.

Part of the vibrational frequency of a crystal comes from its color, and various colors are associated with different vibrations, which are, in turn, associated with different healing properties. In general, the colors of crystals correspond with chakras in the human energy system. Following is a basic primer on colors and their properties. You can choose any crystal with these colors, and it will have a vibration that aligns with the properties mentioned below.

BLACK

Black is associated with the root chakra. In fêng shui, it is associated with the element of water and has yin, or passive and feminine, energies. It has the following properties:

- grounds
- absorbs unwanted energies
- provides protective energy

There are many black healing crystals, including:

- Apache tears
- astrophyllite
- black opal
- black tourmaline
- Boji Stones (Kansas Pop Rocks)
- hematite
- jasper
- jet
- obsidian
- onyx
- shungite
- smoky quartz (dark)
- sphalerite
- tektites

A friend was over at my house recently, and I gave him a piece of a high-vibration stone called Super Seven to hold. The vibration of Super Seven pulls you into higher realms, so it can be challenging the first time you come in contact with it. The piece he held was a substantial chunk, and he immediately got lightheaded and dizzy. I had him sit down and handed him a piece of black tourmaline. It grounded him, and he felt better right away.

One of the crystal shops I visit frequently has a "grounding chair" because often being in proximity to many high-vibration crystals can feel disorienting. The chair has black stones taped underneath its seat, and when someone notices lightheadedness or disorientation, they can sit in the chair to ground the energy.

RED

Red is also associated with the first chakra, which deals with issues of safety, security, foundation, and groundedness. In fêng shui, red is associated with the element of fire, and within the balance of yin and yang, it is yang: active and masculine. The color red is associated with the following qualities:

- promotes passion
- grounds
- enhances feelings of safety and security
- warms
- energizes
- supports loyalty

There are numerous red crystals you can choose from, including:

- bloodstone
- cinnabar
- coral
- garnet
- heliotrope
- pyrope
- red carnelian
- red hematite
- red jasper
- red onyx
- red opal
- rhodonite
- rubellite tourmaline
- ruby
- sardonyx
- spinel
- vanadinite

Fêng shui recommends having a little, but not too much, of the color red in the marital bedroom to stoke the fires of passion. Having too much, however, can be too energizing and may hamper sleep with its active energies. Therefore, a small red stone of an inch or less, such as a small garnet, on a dresser in your master bedroom can help keep your marriage or relationship passionate and alive.

In a recent consultation with one of my students, she shared she was struggling with low energy and finding passion for much of anything in her life. I suggested she find a red crystal, such as a piece of red hematite or a garnet, and start meditating with it while focusing on the things she didn't feel passionate about any longer. She later shared with me that meditating with the crystal helped reignite her fire within a few days.

BROWN

Brown is associated with the second (sacral) chakra, which relates to creativity, enjoyment, and understanding your place within various groups, such as society, family, and friends. In fêng shui, it is associated with the elements of wood and earth. Wood is yang (active and masculine), and it represents growth, expansion, and vitality. Earth is yin (passive and feminine), and it represents balance and grounding. Balance and harmony of both yin and yang are essential for well-being, as lack of balance leads to dis-harmony, which can lead to dis-ease and lack of wellness, so brown is an important color because it promotes this harmony. Certain brown stones, such as petrified wood, are more likely to support the wood element, while others, such as fossils and smoky quartz, support the earth element. Brown crystals may have the following properties:

- assists with integration of energy

- grounds

- helps you connect to the natural world

- balances

- supports vitality

- strengthens

There are several brown crystals, including the following:

- amber (dark)
- ammonite fossils
- Botswana agate
- bronzite
- cacoxanite
- jasper, picture jasper
- petrified wood
- pietersite
- smoky amethyst
- smoky citrine
- smoky quartz
- stromatolite
- tigers eye (dark)
- topaz

I keep a dark brown smoky quartz in my workspace to help keep me grounded and focused when I work. When I don't have it nearby, I often struggle with staying focused.

My husband is on the autism spectrum (formerly Asperger's syndrome). His neurological differences have led to experiential differences from people who are neurotypical, and he has often felt like an outsider, not just in society as a whole but within subgroups of society as well, such as in his workplace, in his family, and among groups of friends. This has led to a poor understanding of his place within various groups, which is a second-chakra issue. In recent months, Jim has been drawn to ammonite fossils, petrified wood, and picture jasper. As he's added to his collection and worked with each of these elements regularly, I've noticed a change. He's started to examine his belief and understanding about his place within groups, recognizing that he is more connected to others than he previously understood. He's also gained valuable insights about how he does fit in and why that plays a valuable role within each group he is a part of. This has changed not only his experience but also how he relates to those within his circles, and he says he has a new sense of belonging.

When Jim started collecting these brown stones, it wasn't with any intent to change anything in his life. He was intuitively drawn to them, and he liked how they looked. So even without his intention to bring about changes, by following his interest and intuition and collecting them, they have greatly enhanced his understanding of who he is.

ORANGE

Orange is also associated with the second (sacral) chakra, which is about creativity, a sense of self, and integrity. Similar to brown stones, it's also associated with prosperity and an understanding of one's place within groups. In fêng shui, it is associated with the element of fire, which is yang, masculine, and active. Qualities of orange crystals include:

- supports creative flow and ideas

- facilitates processes

- promotes integrity

- assists with self-definition

- balances personal power

- helps with control issues

- supports sexuality

- assists with decision making

- affects prosperity or lack thereof

There are many orange crystals you can choose from, including:

- amber (medium)

- aragonite

- carnelian

- coral

- fire agate

- fire opal

- orange calcite

- orange labradorite

- peach moonstone

- Siberian gold quartz

- sunstone

- vanadinite

- zincite

A few weeks after my dad's funeral, I was struggling to find my groove again. I tend to be a sunny, optimistic person, but losing my dad knocked me for a loop. One day I stopped at my favorite crystal shop. They had a beautiful necklace made from Siberian gold quartz and golden labradorite. I was immediately drawn to it, even though I never wear orange. I purchased it, and wearing it lifted my spirits significantly. It continues to do so, and it helped me return to my normal sunny optimism after a difficult period.

YELLOW

Yellow is associated with the third chakra, which is the center of self-esteem and self-identity. In fêng shui, yellow and represents money and wealth, and it is also associated with the elements of metal, such as with the color gold, and earth, which is yellow. Metal is yin, which is passive and feminine, and it has the attributes of strength, determination, and ambition. Earth is also yin, and it represents balance and grounding.

Attributes of yellow stones include:

- enhances self-worth and self-esteem

- supports prosperity and abundance

- provides a sense of belonging

- imparts courage

- strengthens personal honor

There are many yellow crystals you can choose from, including:

- amber (light)
- bismuth
- chrysoberyl
- citrine
- golden labradorite
- golden selenite
- healer quartz
- heliodor
- pyrite
- rutile
- spessartite garnet
- sulfur
- sunstone
- topaz
- yellow labradorite
- yellow tigers eye

Back before I had much knowledge about crystals, I befriended a shaman who started teaching me about them. At the time, I felt beaten down by life—unhappy in my job, exhausted, sick, and just generally not moving in a direction I wanted to go. I had self-esteem issues, and at my shaman friend's recommendation, I started wearing tigers eye on a long chain around my neck.

Slowly I started to feel better about myself. While much of my situation hadn't yet changed, I felt lighter and happier. My self-esteem started to grow from wearing that crystal, and it was another powerful reminder telling me I was on the right track with learning about crystals and healing.

GREEN

Green is associated with the fourth chakra, the heart chakra, which is the center of kindness, compassion, unconditional love, and forgiveness. In fêng shui, the color green is associated with the wood element, which is yang, or active and masculine, and it also promotes health and wealth. Other properties of green crystals include the following:

- promotes love
- strengthens compassion
- allows forgiveness
- fosters kindness
- promotes selflessness
- tempers grief
- calms anger
- alleviates self-centeredness

Because of their association with unconditional love and compassion, green crystals are among my favorites, and there are many you can choose from, including:

- amazonite
- aventurine
- chlorite
- chrysoberyl
- chrysocolla
- chrysoprase
- dioptase
- emerald
- epidote
- fluorite
- goshenite
- green apatite
- green obsidian
- green tourmaline
- heliotrope
- jade
- malachite
- moldavite
- moss agate
- peridot
- prehnite
- seraphinite

My husband had a mild heart attack a few years ago, and it helped both of us realize how much suppressed anger he was carrying. Repressed anger and resentment can block love and thus cause heart chakra imbalance, and some studies suggest repressed anger is a factor in causing heart disease. We knew he had to learn to release the anger if he was to heal and protect his heart in the future. We began working with malachite and green fluorite, and he started wearing a pendant of green fluorite over his heart chakra. It helped to temper some of his anger and release it, and he reacts less angrily to life events now and is calmer and more even-tempered.

PINK

Pink is also associated with the heart chakra and issues of kindness, love, and compassion. In Western culture, it is considered a feminine receptive color, but in fêng shui, it is associated with the element of fire (which is masculine, active, and yang). These color association differences are cultural, and these cultural associations create an assumption of properties. Your intention when using pink can help resolve associated issues. Pink is also the color of romantic love and commitment. Qualities associated with pink gemstones include:

- promotes love
- fosters forgiveness
- activates kindness
- strengthens compassion

Pink stones are plentiful, and you can choose from the following:

- danburite
- fluorite
- kunzite
- morganite
- pink tourmaline
- rhodochrosite
- rhodonite
- rose quartz
- rubellite tourmaline
- ruby
- stilbite

A few years ago, I became enchanted with the pink stone morganite. From the moment I found some, I felt it radiating a calming, peaceful, loving energy. I bought two pieces and brought them home. Shortly after I bought some, a friend came over to my house. He was experiencing relationship problems. Suddenly I knew why I'd purchased a second piece of morganite in spite of its price. I gave him a piece. I recently spent some time with him and his partner, and they are happy together. The morganite has been healing.

BLUE

Blue is associated with the fifth, or throat, chakra, which is about speaking your truth and expressing yourself, as well as the creative expression of ideas. In fêng shui, it is associated with the element of water, which is passive, receptive, feminine, and yin. The water element also reflects softness and flexibility, and too much can stimulate anxiety. Other attributes associated with blue stones include:

- enhances communication
- facilitates speaking your truth
- promotes integrity
- fosters honesty
- alleviates judgment
- calms criticism
- fosters self-expression

Blue crystals you can use include:

- angelite
- apatite
- aquamarine
- azurite
- blue calcite
- blue fluorite
- blue kyanite
- blue lace agate
- blue tigers eye
- blue topaz
- blue zircon
- celestite
- chalcedony
- dumortierite
- fluorite
- iolite
- kyanite
- labradorite
- lapis lazuli
- larimar
- sapphire
- sodalite
- tanzanite
- turquoise

My most profound experience with blue crystals was when the first practitioner I went to who used crystals placed them on my throat. I also keep blue calcite (which is also known as the student's stone) front and center when I teach my classes to help improve communication and learning throughout the class.

INDIGO, PURPLE, AND VIOLET

Indigo, purple, and violet stones are associated with the sixth, or third eye, chakra, which is the chakra of reasoning, intuition, and higher guidance. In fêng shui, purple is associated with communication with higher realms, as well as with the element of fire, which is active, masculine, and yang. Qualities of purple stones include:

- strengthens intuition

- supports relationship with higher self

- facilitates open- or closed-mindedness

- fosters intellect

- supports critical thinking

- enhances emotional intelligence

- strengthens trust in a higher power

- promotes better sleep

- helps with sobriety

Purple crystals are among my favorites in my healing work because they enhance intuition, and there are many available, including:

- amethyst

- charoite

- fluorite

- kunzite

- labradorite

- lepidolite

- sugilite

- tanzanite

I have a friend who is just starting to recognize her intuitive abilities. As she is going through a difficult time in her life (a divorce from her high school sweetheart), she's also starting to notice her intuition is sharpening and she is receiving psychic information. Often, abilities like these come to the fore during periods of change, and this seems to be the case with her.

Right now, she feels as if she lacks control of these abilities, so I gave her a piece of charoite. The stone called to me when I was in a crystal shop, and it helped me stay focused on what was important in my life during a tumultuous period. It felt appropriate to pass it on to her. As it provided balance to me, my hope is it will provide balance and insight for her as she goes through this change in her life.

WHITE AND CLEAR

White and clear crystals are very high vibration crystals that are associated with the seventh, or crown, chakra, which connects you to higher realms and guides you on a spiritual path. Other attributes include:

- supports connection to the Divine

- enhances ethics and values

- promotes universal trust

- strengthens connection to all that is

- strengthens empathy

- promotes spirituality

- enhances understanding of your greater spiritual nature

There are a number of white and clear crystals, including:

- apophyllite
- azezulite
- chrysanthemum stone
- clear quartz
- danburite
- diamond
- dolomite
- goshenite
- Herkimer diamond
- howlite

- lemurian seed quartz
- moonstone
- natrolite
- opal
- pearl
- phenacite
- scolecite
- selenite
- snowflake obsidian

My go-to clear crystal is clear quartz because it not only has a high vibration, but it also amplifies any energy it comes in contact with. It's often the first crystal I recommend people purchase because it is plentiful, affordable, and versatile.

On the other end of the spectrum, the crystal I like to recommend to people who are experienced with crystals and seeking a higher vibrational experience is phenacite. The crystal has an incredibly high vibration that makes you feel lightheaded if you're not prepared for it. It's great to use in meditation when you want to contact higher realms, and some of the best guidance I receive in my meditations come when I am wearing or holding phenacite.

MULTICOLORED

Many crystals have multiple colors. These are excellent for aura cleansing, chakra balancing, and working on more than one issue at a time. The properties vary depending on the individual colors in each crystal and the type of crystal it is. Look to each color in the crystal for more insight.

Some common multicolored crystals include:

- alexandrite

- ametrine

- bismuth

- Dalmatian jasper

- mookite jasper

- ocean jasper

- rainbow fluorite

- rainbow moonstone

- rainbow obsidian

- ruby in fuchsite

- ruby in zoisite

- snowflake obsidian

- watermelon tourmaline

43

Opacity

Whether a crystal is opaque or transparent also affects its healing properties. Opaque crystals (such as jasper and malachite) absorb excess energy, while transparent crystals (such as clear quartz or amethyst) amplify energies. Therefore, if you are working with an excess of energy like overindulgence or too much energy flow, such as in a condition like high blood pressure, an opaque crystal can help absorb the excesses in order to rebalance the energies. On the other hand, if you have a shortage of energy or an energetic blockage, such as in the case of congestive heart failure or low physical stamina, a clear crystal can help amplify the energy and increase energetic flow to clear the blockage.

In my classes, I use the (somewhat gross but concrete and easy-to-understand) example of diarrhea and constipation. Diarrhea is a condition of excess and too much flow; you'd use an opaque crystal here to absorb excess. On the other hand, constipation is a condition of not enough flow and blockage. A clear colored crystal is used here to amplify and get energy moving again. Another example is overeating versus anorexia. Overeating is a behavior of excess energy and could therefore benefit from an opaque crystal, while anorexia is a behavior of low energy and could benefit from a clear crystal.

You can also use crystals in various color combinations to support different energies (see chapter 14, "Using Crystals in Combinations"). Since many issues in life aren't the result of one simple process or difficulty, combining crystal colors and opacities can help resolve complex issues where multiple energies come into play.

Enhancing Energy with Color and Opacity

Color has a much stronger effect on physical, spiritual, emotional, and mental well-being than many people realize. By carefully selecting the colors of the crystals you use to correspond with your energy anatomy, in this case primarily chakras, and by tailoring the opacity of the crystal to help provide energetic balance, you can carefully target specific issues to help bring about resolution that serves the highest and greatest good.

CHAPTER 3

Lattice Patterns

When crystals grow, they form an internal structure and order that geologists refer to as a "crystal lattice system." There are six main lattice systems for healing crystals: monoclinic, triclinic, orthorhombic, tetragonal, hexagonal, and cubic. In healing crystals, we also refer to a seventh system for all those "crystals" that don't meet the technical definition. This seventh system is called amorphous, and it is a catchall for the noncrystalline healing crystals.

Metaphysically, each of the crystal lattice patterns has a type of vibrational energy, and gaining an understanding of how each of these lattice structures affects energy and vibration can help you be even more targeted in your crystal selection. This will allow you to choose crystals with confidence, knowing they have all the properties necessary to support your intention to bring about specific changes.

Monoclinic

Monoclinic crystals are protective. Their vibration supports an expansion of energies, so they are good crystals to work with when your main objective is growth in any area of your life.

Crystals in this category include the following:

- acanthite
- azurite
- borax
- charoite
- chlorite
- chrysocolla
- cryolite
- desert rose
- diopside
- epidote
- gypsum
- hiddenite
- howlite
- jadeite
- kunzite
- lazulite
- lepidolite
- malachite
- manganite
- moonstone
- muscovite (mica)
- petalite
- scolecite
- selenite
- serpentine
- talc
- tremolite
- wolframite

A friend was looking to expand the energy of unconditional love in his life with the goal of growing as an energy healer who acted from a place of love as opposed to ego. He felt that in his healing sessions, he was ego focused and thus making choices that had to do with his personal wishes for himself and his clients instead of those things that served his clients' highest and greatest good, and he wanted to come from a purer heart space where his own personal filters didn't affect his healing abilities.

With that in mind, he asked me how he could expand that love energy in his life using crystals, moving from ego to heart. I recommended kunzite, which is a pinkish purple monoclinic crystal that is well known for growing and expanding the capacity for unconditional love. What's interesting is even before I recommended kunzite, my friend felt drawn to it. He started meditating with kunzite and using it in his healing work, and he reported he noticed an immediate shift in his focus during his healing sessions into a heart space instead of working from a place of ego.

Triclinic

Triclinic crystals repel unwanted energies, and they help contain energies you'd like to maintain. They are also energetic balancers, so you can use them whenever you feel an imbalance in any of your life forces, energies, or emotions. These are good crystals to turn to when your life feels out of balance.

Crystals in this category include the following:

- amazonite
- amblygonite
- aventurine
- axenite
- feldspar
- kyanite
- labradorite
- larimar
- magnesite
- rhodonite
- sunstone
- turquoise

I have a student who is empathic. He is frequently deeply affected by the energies of other people, experiencing their emotions as his own, and he's also susceptible to being overwhelmed by high levels of energy. This can make day-to-day life a struggle because he finds it difficult to focus and go about his business without being overwhelmed by everyone else's energy.

I purchased a blue kyanite pendant, which is a triclinic crystal, for him to wear. He wears it on a chain around his neck and reports he feels better able to focus and less overwhelmed when he wears it. This has been helpful for him both at work and in his personal relationships. The kyanite is serving to repel and protect him from the energies and emotions around him, and it also helps him find more balance between his own emotions and those of others.

Orthorhombic

Orthorhombic crystals vibrate at an energy that removes blockages, clears, and cleanses. They can help release you when you are in stuck patterns of thoughts, beliefs, or behaviors. They can also help if you are feeling blocked creatively or in other aspects of your life.

Included in this lattice system are the following:

- abalone
- alexandrite
- angelite
- aragonite
- celestite
- chrysoberyl
- chrysocolla
- danburite
- dumortierite
- hemimorphite
- iolite
- peridot
- prehnite
- tanzanite
- topaz
- zoisite

A few years ago, I struggled with fibroids. They caused many issues, and at one point, I had to have an emergency blood transfusion and surgery because of them. Fibroids are related to blocked energy in the second chakra. At the same time, I felt creatively and professionally blocked, which is also a second-chakra issue.

I started meditating daily with aragonite, an orthorhombic crystal, focusing on allowing energy to flow freely through that area. Within a few weeks, the issues associated with the fibroids cleared up, and I suddenly found a new direction for my writing that felt more authentic. The aragonite helped cleanse and clear the blockages I was experiencing in my second chakra to restore balance both physically and creatively.

Tetragonal

Tetragonal crystals are attractors. They can help you attract certain energies into your life. They also transmute negative energy to positive, block negative energy, and amplify positive energy. These are the crystals you use when you wish to change the energy of a situation or when you wish to attract something new into your life.

Crystals in this lattice system include the following:

- apophyllite
- chalcopyrite
- rutile
- scapolite
- scheelite
- vesuvianite
- wulfenite
- zircon

Last year I decided I wanted the opportunity to teach more classes and be part of a larger community of energy healers and metaphysicians. At the time, I taught four or five classes per year, and what I really wanted to do was teach monthly. I thought I'd found a place locally to start teaching each month with a group of like-minded individuals, but the owner's lease fell through, so I was once again left trying to find the perfect situation.

With the intention of attracting a location where I could teach monthly classes alongside a group of others with similar focus, I dug a piece of apophyllite (a tetragonal crystal) out of my stash and placed it near my workstation. Shortly thereafter, one of my friends contacted me to tell me he wanted to start offering metaphysical classes and events through his studio in Portland, Oregon, which is about an hour away but has a much larger population to draw from than the tiny town where I live. I started teaching classes there last fall, and I teach at least monthly as part of a group of like-minded individuals. We have formed a collective of teachers and practitioners with a common goal of raising energetic vibrations, called Vision Collective, and we've even moved into a larger studio space.

The apophyllite combined with my intention helped me to attract the exact situation I was seeking.

Hexagonal

Hexagonal (also called rhombohedral) crystals are energizers and manifestors. They bring energy and improve vitality. They also amplify. These are good crystals to use when you wish to increase certain energies or manifest things in your life. They work well with goal setting, intention, affirmation, and visualization. The hexagonal system of crystals also includes trigonal crystals, which you'll sometimes see listed separately, but for healing work, trigonal and hexagonal crystals facilitate the same types of energy.

Crystals in the hexagonal family include the following:

- agate
- amethyst
- apatite
- aquamarine
- beryl
- bismuth
- calcite
- chalcedony
- chaoite
- cinnabar
- citrine
- corundum (sapphire, ruby)
- dioptase
- dolomite
- emerald
- hematite
- jasper
- magnesite
- morganite
- oregonite
- phenacite
- quartz
- schorl (tourmaline)
- sugilite
- vanadinite
- zincite

Several years ago with my son months away from heading off to college, I realized I needed to step up my business and earn more money. I'd been working as a freelance writer for many years and had also authored a few books, but the amount of money my husband and I were going to need to send the kiddo to college without experiencing a huge strain on our finances was a lot more than I was bringing in. At the time, one of my freelance jobs was writing for an online company that helped rehabilitate people's online reputations, and to me, the job felt icky because many of the people deserved the Internet reputations they had earned.

I knew I needed to manifest different jobs that focused on bringing healing to the world instead but that allowed me to make enough money to pay for my son's education. I'd heard green crystals could increase wealth (because they were the color of money in our culture). I happened to have some dioptase (a green, hexagonal crystal). Each day, I held it in my lap as I wrote affirmations about the types of jobs I was seeking. Within a few months, I was presented with the opportunity to write cookbooks for people with specific health conditions that contained healing foods. Cooking is a passion of mine, and I've always focused on helping people to find ways to heal physically, mentally, emotionally, and spiritually, so this was right up my alley. Writing those books has been deeply fulfilling and has allowed us to support my son while he is away at university. Doing affirmations with a hexagonal crystal helped to manifest work I loved that paid what I needed.

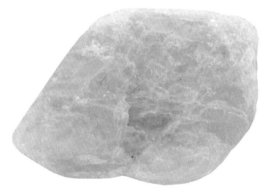

Cubic (Isometric)

You'll sometimes see the cubic system referred to as isometric. These are crystals that are used to improve physical situations. They are also good crystals for grounding energies, and they can stabilize energy and situations. For example, if a situation feels charged or unstable, cubic crystals can help.

Included in this lattice structure are the following crystals:

- copper
- diamond
- fluorite
- galena
- garnet
- gold
- halite

- hessonite
- magnetite
- pyrite
- silver
- sodalite
- spessartine
- spinel

I tend to not be grounded. In fact, for years I described that I felt I didn't live in my body but hovered above it. I also experienced many health issues because I didn't inhabit my body, and I often lacked focus. I lost my keys a lot. It happened several times a day usually; my family still teases me about it.

I knew I needed to move back into my body and ground myself, for both my health and my focus, so I started wearing red garnet, which is a red cubic stone known for being grounding. Each morning, I would also hold a garnet and visualize roots growing from my feet into the earth in an attempt to ground myself more. I noticed I was inhabiting my body more. I bumped into things less frequently, my health improved, and I got better about not losing my keys.

55

While I still have a tendency to not be grounded, I know that when I get too drifty, I can work with a garnet or wear one, and I'll settle back into my body and be better able to focus.

Amorphous

Amorphous crystals don't actually refer to a crystalline lattice structure, but rather are a catchall for other substances classified as healing crystals. Therefore, properties in this group vary. Healing crystals included in this group are:

- amber
- Apache tears
- bronzite
- fossils
- lapis lazuli
- moldavite
- pearl
- petrified wood
- obsidian
- opal
- orgonite (orgone)
- tektite

Amorphous crystals have various properties, mostly related to their color and shape. I give Apache tears to my grieving friends and suggest amber for people struggling with sadness because it is a warm and happy crystal. My friend Tristan swears moldavite jumps in his hand and brings him to higher consciousness. My friend Mackenna carries bronzite with her for grounding.

Each of these "crystals" carries healing properties, but these are based on the individual crystal, so in general I recommend looking up their properties if you're seeking a specific recommendation.

The Value of Lattice

Knowing a crystal's lattice structure can help solidify your intention when using the crystal. While lattice is secondary to color and opacity in crystal selection, when you have a particular target in mind, knowing the crystal's lattice pattern can help you choose the right crystal to meet your specific desires for healing and change.

CHAPTER 4

Shapes of Crystals

When you first walk into a crystal shop, you'll see a rainbow of vivid crystals in a variety of shapes. Polished stones sit alongside points, clusters, wands, and even crystals cut into specific geometric shapes. And just as you may be drawn to a crystal's energy or color, you can also be drawn to its shape. For example, I often find myself drawn to rough stones and clusters, while my husband tends to be drawn to stones that have been polished and shaped. This may be because we each have specific needs, and our intuition is showing us the best way to meet those needs through particular shapes.

This is because the shape of a crystal can also affect its energy. The shape refers to how crystals are cut and finished, as well as the form they are in. For example, are they raw or polished, clusters or points? The crystal's shape effects are secondary, however. In general, color, opacity, and lattice system are much stronger determinants of how the crystals will function for healing purposes.

Raw Versus Polished

You'll find crystals predominately take two forms: raw crystals and polished crystals. Raw crystals are in their natural state. They typically have a rough exterior and may take natural forms, such as clusters or points. Raw crystals look like rocks, pulled from the earth. On the other hand, polished crystals have been tumbled and are typically smooth and shiny.

People frequently ask me if there is a difference between the energy in raw crystals versus polished crystals. My answer is it depends on whom you ask. Some people find the energy of raw crystals feels more powerful, while others claim polished crystals do. I have and use both and don't find much of a difference, so it's really up to personal preference. Go with what feels most appropriate to you for any situation.

Geometric Shapes

Some crystals are cut into specific geometric shapes, while others are left in more natural shapes. In this section, I'll discuss some of the shapes and their properties.

POINTS

Crystal points refer to a terminated point on one or both ends. The point may be natural, or it may be shaped through carving and cleaving.

The wide end of a point gathers energy, while the narrow end directs energy (think of an upside-down funnel, with the base being widest). Use crystals with this shape to direct energy to a specific location. For example, if you place clear quartz points around the outside of a grid with the points facing outward, they are drawing the energy from the grid and directing it into the surrounding environment. Similarly, if you place the narrow points so they face into the grid, you are drawing energy from the environment into the grid.

I use points to direct energy, particularly in grids, which are groupings of crystals deliberately placed in sacred geometrical shapes to energize specific intentions (see chapter 14 for more about grids). I may also use a point to gather and direct energy in a room or space. For example, I like to do this with clear quartz, which is an energetic amplifier. I have a clear quartz pointed at my prosperity corner in my house with the wide end pointed toward the rest of my home to amplify that energy in my life and home. So the point gathers the energy of prosperity from the corner, and the wide end disperses it throughout my home, as if I am funneling the energy from one small area and widely distributing it through a wider space.

CLUSTERS

Clusters are naturally occurring groups of points. For example, you can often find clear quartz clusters that are connected to a common base with points extending in every direction.

Clusters direct vibration throughout a space, creating a diffuse energy. They are good for filling an entire room or space with energy. Use them in areas where you'd like the whole place to be filled with that crystal's frequency.

I have an amethyst cluster in my bedroom. Amethyst is well known for promoting restful sleep and fighting insomnia, so I allow its calming energy to fill my bedroom.

WANDS

Wands are generally carved, elongated cylinders with either rounded or pointed ends. They are good for directing energy to something specific. They are often used in massage or energy healing to direct crystal energy to a particular point. I have a selenite wand that has a crystal for each chakra on its surface. I use it to help balance the energies of all the chakras. I do this in one of two ways—either by pointing the wand at a specific chakra and using the wide end to gather universal energy to direct it to that chakra, or by placing it on its side along the midline of my body near the heart chakra with the point pointing toward my crown chakra to move energy upward from the earth or pointing toward my root chakra to direct the energy from crown to root. Which direction I use—root to crown or crown to root—depends on what I am intuitively guided to do. For instance, on days when I am not feeling grounded, I point it toward my root chakra, while on days I need to be energized or inspired, I point it toward my crown chakra.

SPHERES

Spheres are one of the common ways you'll find crystals cut and shaped. They are also some of the most popular shaped stones. When shaped like spheres, crystals send diffuse energy and support oneness and wholeness. They also balance and harmonize.

For example, you might choose a sphere to harmonize energy in an area of the home where a disharmony has occurred, such as in a marital bedroom following a divorce. I have a sphere of ibis jasper in my living room next to a spot where I enjoy unwinding because ibis jasper is excellent for generating relaxation, and its shape will diffuse and harmonize the energy throughout the space.

TETRAHEDRONS

A tetrahedron is more commonly referred to as a pyramid. It is a three-dimensional shape with four triangular faces. Tetrahedrons are associated with the element of fire. They also balance, manifest, and support creativity, and gather and direct energy.

I have a lapis tetrahedron in my creative space to help support creative expression. I gave a friend a tigers eye tetrahedron to help him maintain a balanced sense of self during recent relationship difficulties.

HEXAHEDRONS

You may know one type of hexahedron by its more common name, a cube. It can also be an elongated (rectangular) block. It may also have similar shapes without the 90-degree angles, so a hexahedron may be a three-dimensional trapezoid or a pyramid without the top point. Hexahedrons have six faces.

Crystals cut in these shapes support the element of earth. They are grounding, energizing, and stabilizing, and support improved focus. For example, a student may want to place a piece of blue calcite, which is known as the student's stone, cut into a hexahedron in a study area to support good study habits. If you aren't grounded, it may be helpful to meditate with a black or red hexahedron.

OCTAHEDRONS

Octahedrons have eight triangular faces. A diamond is an example of an octahedron.

Octahedrons support the element of air. They promote unconditional love, compassion, and nurturing. You often find green fluorite cut into octahedrons. Green fluorite is a stone of love, and when cut into an octahedron, it strengthens the energy of unconditional love and compassion. If you are struggling to forgive someone or to find compassion for another, then this is an excellent cut and stone that can help you do so.

DODECAHEDRONS

Dodecahedrons have 12 flat faces. They are complex shapes that look like a 12-sided die. They support the element of ethers and help achieve connection to the higher self and the Divine. They also help tune you in to higher guidance, strengthen psychic ability, and raise your vibrational frequency.

A high-frequency stone such as phenacite or clear quartz cut into a dodecahedron and placed in a meditation space can enhance guidance. If you are trying to enhance psychic abilities, carrying an amethyst cut into a dodecahedron can support this by helping you tune in to intuitive insight.

ICOSAHEDRONS

An icosahedron has 20 flat faces. It may look like a more complex many-sided die, or it may look like a star with multiple points interspersed evenly around the outside.

Icosahedrons support the element of water. They are associated with change, flow, and movement, and they promote integrity, heal sexuality, and foster creativity. Due to the complexity of cutting involved in an icosahedron, these may be more difficult to come by than less complex shapes. However, you can find them. If you do, they are helpful for improving the flow of your life in any area. For example, if you are feeling creatively blocked, then a carnelian icosahedron in your space where you create may remove whatever impedes you. A garnet icosahedron placed on a bedside table can help you overcome issues associated with sexuality.

So Many Shapes

These are the most common shapes in which you'll find crystals. There are many others as well, including egg shapes, crystals cut into the shapes of animals, crystals formed into trees and flowers, and gems cut into specific shapes for jewelry. Listen to what your intuition tells you. If you gravitate to a certain shape or cut, chances are there is something about its energy you need in your life. While you can choose shapes deliberately to affect change, always listen to your internal guidance to direct you to crystals in the shapes you need the most.

CHAPTER 5

Crystals and the Human Energy System

It's impossible to separate body, mind, and spirit. All three of these aspects make up the whole of you, and each affects your physical, spiritual, mental, and emotional health. All are affected by the experiences you have and how you choose to respond to them. Therefore, when one of these aspects experiences an imbalance, it affects your system as a whole. As I discussed earlier, the vibration of crystals can affect the vibration of the human energy system by the principle of entrainment, which is when oscillating bodies in proximity to one another move into phase and vibrate at the same frequency. Because of this, crystals can help remove blockages or balance energies that affect your body, mind, and spirit. By rebalancing your energy body, you may experience healing in body, mind, and spirit as well.

There are various components to your energy anatomy. While I won't go too far into depth about energy anatomy, I do want to give you at least a basis for understanding it. Part 3 of this book will go into more depth about how to direct a crystal's energy so it affects your energy in specific ways.

Aura

The idea of the human auric field first appeared in theosophical literature around the turn of the 20th century. Since then, a belief in auras has come to be widely accepted among energy healers, metaphysicians, and mystics.

Everything has an aura. The aura is the energetic structure that emanates from you and surrounds you. Your aura reflects your current state of emotional, physical, mental, and spiritual health, and its colors can change from day to day or even moment to moment. Some people can see auras. The art of Kirlian photography allows you to see an aura, which is multiple colors and has many layers extending outward from your body and surrounding you.

Crystals I like to use for aura cleansing include:

- multicolored crystals, like rainbow fluorite, or those that have a multicolored flash, like opals or moonstone, that have all of the chakra colors to balance energy throughout the body

- snowflake obsidian, which connects the root chakra to the crown chakra to allow aura cleansing

- spirit quartz, which is a form of amethyst that has small crystal "prickles" on it and is sometimes also called cactus quartz; the points face in multiple directions to move energy throughout your aura

- selenite, which is one of the most cleansing crystals available (I use it to cleanse other crystals); waving a selenite wand through the auric field can help cleanse and balance the energy

69

Chakras

The concept of chakra energy centers is ancient, with their earliest mentions appearing in early Hindu texts (between about 1500 and 500 BCE), called *The Vedas*. You can also find discussion of chakras in yoga, Buddhism, and Jainism.

Chakras are the energetic connection between your physical and etheric (energetic or spiritual) bodies. Your physical body is made up of your skin, bones, organs, and fluids, as well as your thoughts and beliefs. Your etheric body consists of your energy, your spirituality, your emotions, and your connection to higher realms. These diverse aspects of you meet in your chakras. Your body is physical, as is the thinking, rational part of your mind. The emotional part of your mind and your spirit are etheric in nature. Chakras connect these into one whole.

You have seven main chakra energy centers running through your body along the spinal column. According to yogis and various ancient belief systems, your chakras are associated with specific energies, body parts, and emotional, mental, and spiritual issues.

ROOT CHAKRA

Color. Red

Location. Base of your spine

Related physical areas. Legs, feet, base of spine, rectum, tailbone

Emotional, mental, and spiritual qualities. Safety and security, grounding and protection, oneness and connection to others, family loyalty, abandonment, standing up for yourself

Crystals. Red and black crystals, garnet, Boji Stones, obsidian, snowflake obsidian, ruby

Root Chakra
Basic Trust

SACRAL CHAKRA

Color. Orange

Location. A few inches below your navel

Related physical areas. Lower back, sexual organs, hips and pelvis, organs of the lower abdomen

Emotional, mental, and spiritual qualities. Personal integrity, personal power, self-identity, prosperity, control

Crystals. Orange and brown crystals, smoky quartz, carnelian, aragonite

Sacral Chakra
Sexuality, Creativity

SOLAR PLEXUS CHAKRA

Color. Yellow

Location. Bottom of your sternum

Related physical areas. Upper abdomen, stomach, upper intestines, pancreas, gallbladder, liver, adrenals, mid-back

Emotional, mental, and spiritual qualities. Personality, self-worth and self-esteem, separation from tribal and family identity, social conditioning, honor within a society or tribe, courage, maturity

Crystals. Yellow and gold crystals, citrine, pyrite, yellow tigers eye

Solar Plexus
Wisdom, Power

HEART CHAKRA

Color. Green

Location. Center of your chest

Related physical areas. Heart, lungs, ribs, upper back, arms, shoulders, hands, circulatory system, diaphragm, breathing

Emotional, mental, and spiritual qualities. Unconditional love, anger, forgiveness, compassion, balance, strength, connection of physical to mental and spiritual, grief, bitterness, self-centeredness

Crystals. Pink and green crystals, organite, rose quartz, emerald

Heart Chakra
Love, Healing

THROAT CHAKRA

Color. Blue

Location. Over your Adam's apple

Related physical areas. Throat, thyroid and parathyroid, teeth and gums, mouth, jaw

Emotional, mental, and spiritual qualities. Speaking your truth, communication, self-expression, criticism, judgment of self and others

Crystals. Blue and indigo crystals, blue lace agate, chalcedony, celestite

Throat Chakra
Communication

THIRD EYE CHAKRA

Color. Indigo or violet

Location. Center of your forehead

Related physical areas. Head, eyes, ears, brain

Emotional, mental, and spiritual qualities. Intuition, psychic ability, relationship with higher self or the Divine

Crystals. Purple and violet crystals, amethyst, lepidolite, charoite

Third Eye
Awareness

Crown Chakra
Spirituality

CROWN CHAKRA

Color. White or clear

Location. Just above the top of your head

Related physical areas. Systemic issues, skin, bones, muscles

Emotional, mental, and spiritual qualities. Connection to the Divine, compassion, empathy, walking the path of spirit, ethics and values

Crystals. White and clear crystals, clear quartz, howlite, apophyllite

The Body Electric

You are more than just skin, bones, fluids, and organs. You are far more than a collection of cells. You are also energy, emotion, consciousness, and spirit. You cannot separate one of these aspects of self from the others, and when there is an imbalance in one, the whole is affected. Working with crystals can help you integrate these diverse aspects of self so you can function in wholeness, vitality, strength, and energy.

CHAPTER 6

Guide to Choosing Crystals

With the information I've provided in the previous chapters, you now have all the tools you need to choose the right crystal for whatever energy it is you wish to balance, transform, or bring in to your life.

Order of Importance

I've given you a lot of information. You can use a single criterion from the previous chapters or combine them. Below, I've listed the steps in order of importance for selecting a crystal.

1. *Give top priority to crystal color.* Color has the strongest association with crystal use. If you choose the right color crystal, everything else is of secondary importance. So before you do anything else, reflect on the issue you are trying to solve and determine which color will best address this issue.

2. *Next, decide which lattice pattern will best suit your goals.* Once you have a list of crystals in the appropriate color, from that list, you can zero in on the type of energy you'd like to create,

such as manifestation or balance, by selecting a lattice type that creates that energy.

3. *Decide whether there is too much energy flow or not enough and choose the appropriate opacity.* Your next consideration is whether the crystal is opaque or translucent to balance energies. Crystals have varying degrees of opacity. A good rule of thumb to follow is this: The clearer the crystal, the more it will amplify an energy. The opaquer a crystal is, the more energy it will absorb. If you can't decide whether you need to amplify or absorb, choose a crystal that is moderately opaque but you can still see some light shining through it. An opal would be a good example of this.

4. *Shape and type are of secondary importance.* If you'd like to refine further, you can choose a crystal in an appropriate shape, or one that is rough or tumbled.

5. *When in doubt, listen to your intuition.* In all cases, I recommend you follow your intuition. If you are drawn to a crystal, use it.

Some Scenarios for Selecting Crystals

When people consult me about crystals, I find they frequently ask me about the same types of things. Because of this, I have identified a few key areas where many people are looking for improvement, and I will provide scenarios for each of these to show you how to use the information about color, opacity, and lattice pattern to shift energy in each scenario. I'll use these aspects of healing throughout the book to demonstrate various crystal uses. Shape and type are secondary, and I'll mention those that may be beneficial to each situation, but they aren't as important as the three main components (color, lattice pattern, and opacity). The scenarios we will look at include:

- health and wellness

- prosperity and abundance

- self-love and self-esteem

- purpose in career and life

- forgiveness

- love and relationships

It's important to note that the following are just examples, and you can use the information I've provided to explore scenarios far beyond any of these examples by synthesizing the information in a similar manner.

SCENARIO # 1: HEALTH AND WELLNESS

Recently, Pam has noticed she's constantly tired. She feels sluggish and slow-moving. She notices her skin is dry and her hair and nails are brittle. Weight has never been a struggle before, but she's started gaining, and none of her clothes fit any longer. After several months of struggling, Pam visits her doctor. After testing, he diagnoses hypothyroidism and puts Pam on medication. While the medication is helping, Pam notices she still feels symptomatic, and she decides she'd also like to work on her thyroid disorder from an energetic perspective. She turns to crystals.

Before she can select the proper crystal, Pam analyzes her hypothyroidism.

- *Color and chakra:* Hypothyroidism is a disorder of the thyroid, which is in the throat area. The throat chakra is associated with the color blue, so Pam will need a blue crystal.

- *Lattice structure:* Her condition is one of low vitality and energy. Therefore, a crystal that brings energy and vitality is essential. Hexagonal crystals improve vitality and bring energy.

- *Opaque versus transparent:* Hypothyroidism is a disorder of sluggishness; the thyroid is underactive, and all of Pam's symptoms are symptoms of low energy. Therefore, Pam needs to increase the energy in this area. Because of this, she needs a transparent crystal so she can amplify the energy.

- *Shape and type:* Since the issue is in her throat, Pam's best option is to wear the crystal as a necklace since it will be right over the energetic center in need of balancing. While any shape and type of crystal will work here, it's likely she'll get something shaped and polished since she'll be wearing it as jewelry. A sphere will balance energy, while a diamond shape will promote nurturing. A point will direct energy. Any of these shapes would work well.

Putting all of these elements together, Pam needs a transparent blue hexagonal crystal pendant cut into a shape that pleases her or is shaped as a point, diamond, or sphere. Chalcedony and aquamarine are good choices here; both are blue and transparent. Aquamarine tends to be more transparent than chalcedony, so it's likely the best choice for Pam's thyroid condition.

SCENARIO #2: PROSPERITY AND ABUNDANCE

Walt always struggles with money. One week he's up and feeling flush, and the next week he can barely afford to eat. His finances are uneven and a source of stress, and he finds himself worrying about them all the time. He feels like he just can't seem to get ahead; even when he has some extra cash, some major unexpected expense comes along that quickly returns him to the poorhouse. His finances have been uneven his entire life, and he doesn't understand it. He makes good money, but it seems like he can't hold on to it, no matter how hard he tries. It's not that he feels he wants or needs more money; he just needs his finances to be more consistent.

Let's analyze Walt's situation to see which crystal will be of most benefit.

- *Color and chakra:* Prosperity and abundance are second-chakra issues. He can benefit from an orange or brown stone.

- *Lattice structure:* Walt's issue with money is a lack of balance; it's always all or nothing for him. Therefore, he needs a triclinic crystal to help balance his financial situation.

- *Opaque versus transparent:* Cash flow isn't a problem for Walt; he has plenty, and it flows freely, but it also drains away. Likewise, Walt spends an inordinate amount of time worrying about money; this indicates an excess of energy. Walt needs a crystal that is opaque to absorb the excess of energy he puts into thinking and worrying about money.

- *Shape and type:* Because Walt is seeking balance, a sphere is a good option for him, as is a pyramid, but any shape or type can help improve the energy of his situation.

Putting it all together, Walt needs an opaque orange or brown stone with a triclinic lattice structure. An orange aventurine sphere or pyramid is a good choice, and I would suggest that he keep it either in his wallet or in the location where he sits to pay his bills and do his financial planning.

SCENARIO #3: SELF-LOVE AND SELF-ESTEEM

Angela has always struggled with self-esteem. She has a constant dialog going on in the back of her mind that she's simply not good enough; nothing she does is ever enough. When she looks in the mirror, all she sees are thighs that are too big, teeth that are too crooked, and all of her other physical flaws. After socializing, Angela second-guesses herself, going over her interactions moment by moment and cringing at the thought that she laughed too loud, talked too much, or said the wrong thing.

One day, Angela hears her 12-year-old daughter talking about herself in the same way Angela thinks about herself. She realizes her daughter has picked up on her own lack of self-esteem, and Angela wants to set a better example. As she begins to work on her self-esteem, she also decides to do crystal work to support and balance her energy flow around this important issue.

- *Color and chakra:* Self-esteem is a third-chakra issue (the solar plexus), which is associated with the color yellow or gold.

- *Lattice structure:* Angela's low self-esteem is a stuck pattern of thought. Angela needs a crystal that will remove this stuck pattern and encourage new thought patterns, so she'll likely need an orthorhombic crystal here.

- *Opaque versus transparent:* Angela's low self-esteem is a shortage of energy in that area. Therefore, she needs to amplify the energy of self-esteem. She needs a transparent crystal.

- *Shape and type:* Again, shape and type are secondary here. However, an icosahedron, which supports change and flow, may be a good choice if she can find one in this shape.

What Angela needs to help improve her self-esteem is a transparent yellow crystal with an orthorhombic lattice structure. Prehnite, which ranges in color from yellow to green, is a good choice. Angela needs to find prehnite that is on the yellow end of the color spectrum. She can wear it as a long pendant so it falls over her solar plexus, or she can keep it in an area where she spends most of her time. Placing it on a bedside table can also help support developing self-esteem while she sleeps, and meditating with it or holding it while doing affirmations and visualizations for self-esteem can also help.

SCENARIO #4: PURPOSE IN CAREER AND LIFE

Jade feels her life lacks purpose, especially in her career. In college, she drifted from major to major before she dropped out, and as an adult, she changes jobs or careers every few years. It's not that Jade is disinterested in her jobs; it's more that she's interested in everything. It all sounds fascinating, and she has so many skills and abilities she wants to put to work that she gets bored easily and drifts from one thing to another. She is like this in her personal life as well. Everything is interesting. Every type of spirituality is fascinating. But no matter what she discovers, tries, or learns, she feels vaguely dissatisfied, and she'd really like to find "her thing," so she can settle in, focus, and feel as if she is moving forward in life with some type of purpose.

- *Chakra and color:* Jade's intellectual interest in everything and lack of focus are related to her third eye chakra and her mind, or spirit. She needs a crystal that is indigo or violet to facilitate focus.

- *Lattice structure:* Jade needs an energy balancer. Triclinic crystals balance energies and can help her focus in one direction.

- *Transparent versus opaque:* Jade's lack of focus is an overabundance of energy. She has so much energy flowing that she flits from one idea to the next without ever really settling. To improve focus, she needs a crystal that absorbs excess energy, which means she needs an opaque crystal.

- *Shape and type:* Unless she has a specific use, shape and type are of secondary importance here, so any shape or type will do.

What Jade needs is a triclinic crystal in indigo or violet that is opaque. Lavender or indigo labradorite is a good choice. If she can find it carved into a point, Jade can use the wide end to gather energy and the narrow end to focus it. Meditating with the crystal may help improve her focus and help her find her "thing" or sense of purpose.

SCENARIO #5: FORGIVENESS

Andrew can't bring himself to forgive his father, who had always been an inconsistent presence in his life after his parents split up when he was three. When he was 11, his dad married another woman. Andrew's stepmother was mean and sometimes verbally and emotionally abusive, and Andrew's father allowed her to treat Andrew poorly. When his dad had new children, he disappeared from Andrew's life, never even acknowledging birthdays or holidays. Now as an adult in his twenties, Andrew can't bring himself to forgive his father. His anger at his dad occupies a great deal of his mind space, and when the subject of his dad comes up, he feels as if he's being treated poorly all over again, in spite of the fact that he hasn't spoken to his father in six years.

Andrew realizes his anger is holding him back, and he wants to forgive his father so he can move on with his own life.

- *Color and chakra:* Anger and forgiveness are heart chakra issues. Green is associated with the heart chakra as well as with anger, and pink is a color associated with forgiveness and unconditional love.

- *Crystal lattice system:* Tetragonal crystals transmute negative energy into positive. In Andrew's case, they will help transform his anger into forgiveness.

- *Transparent versus opaque:* Andrew has two energies at play here: an overabundance of anger energy and an underabundance of love energy. However, by amplifying his love and forgiveness energy, he can overcome the anger. He needs a transparent crystal that will amplify love and forgiveness.

- *Shape and type:* In this case, finding a crystal carved in a heart shape may be beneficial to further support the development of unconditional love and forgiveness, but this is secondary to the other properties.

With the energies Andrew wants to cultivate, he needs a transparent pink or green tetragonal crystal. If he can find one carved into a heart shape, all the better, but it isn't necessary. The crystal that will meet Andrew's needs is green apophyllite. However, it may be difficult to find apophyllite carved into a heart shape, but a cluster will work well here, too. Andrew can place it in a space where he meditates to create a diffuse energy of unconditional love and healing.

SCENARIO #6: LOVE AND RELATIONSHIPS

It's been years since Sally had a satisfying love relationship. She's already been through two divorces. She's in her late thirties, and she hasn't found anyone who remotely interests her. In the past, she's always chosen partners whom she's found physically attractive, but she didn't necessarily connect with them on an emotional or spiritual level. She wants to change that this time around. Sally wants to attract a mate with whom she has a deep soul connection for a mutually supportive romantic partnership.

- *Color and chakra:* Love and relationships are a heart chakra issue, which is the color green. Further, pink is also a color that supports romantic love and partnership.

- *Lattice structure:* Because she wants to manifest a relationship, Sally will do best with a hexagonal crystal.

- *Transparent versus opaque:* Sally wants to increase the love energy in her life. Therefore, she needs a transparent crystal that will amplify that energy.

- *Shape and type:* Again, shape is secondary here, but the traditional shapes of love and commitment are hearts and diamonds.

Sally can benefit from wearing a crystal over her heart chakra, so a pendant on a long chain shaped as either a heart or a diamond will work. A round or sphere pendant to support oneness or wholeness will also work. She needs an opaque, hexagonal pink or green stone. Traditional stones that work well include the classic stone of romantic and unconditional love, rose quartz. Emeralds and dioptases are also good choices.

Choosing Your Crystal

As you can see from the scenarios above, you can use this system to choose the appropriate crystal for any situation. Once you are able to select the right crystal to cultivate the energy you seek, you need to know how to use it. While I've made a few suggestions for each situation above, there are many more ways you can use crystals to make them a daily part of your life. In the chapters that follow, I discuss the various ways you can harness the energy of the crystals you choose to benefit all aspects of your life.

PART 2

HOW TO LIVE
WITH CRYSTALS

CHAPTER 7

Choosing What Shifts to Focus On

Armed with your basic understanding of selecting crystals based on lattice system, color, opacity, and shape, it's likely you feel ready to head to the crystal store and start buying. Searching for and shopping for crystals is one of my favorite activities; I could do it every day! So I understand the urge to run out and start buying any and all crystals with appeal, and if that's what you wish to do (and you have the budget for it), then go for it.

However, I recommend taking a more focused and targeted approach to your first crystal purchases. By approaching crystal acquisition with intention and care, you can more effectively cultivate the energies you most need in your life.

Crystals have powerful vibration, and they can help change the energy of virtually any situation. While I love change, many people find it stressful. For example, my husband becomes overwhelmed when faced with multiple changes, while I thrive on the adrenaline and chaos it brings. I'm always looking to bring new energy into my life, while he's constantly pumping the brakes to keep things on a more even keel. In this way, each of us balances the other. He brings me moderation, while I encourage him to keep growing. It works for us, and it's helped me realize that taking a moderate approach to change and growth allows me to be more focused and purposeful in the energies I cultivate. In the long term, this more focused shifting of energy has actually facilitated quicker growth.

I've learned from experience that it is possible to be too scattered when trying to shift energetic patterns, and when my approach is scattered instead of focused, the energetic breakthrough I need arrives much more slowly than when I focus on working on just a few issues at a time. Making one or two targeted and effective changes at a time allows you to work with full intention and to integrate those changes into your life more purposefully and thoughtfully.

Where you choose to begin is a personal decision. Many of us, when we contemplate our lives, can come up with dozens of things we'd like to change. However, chances are there are one or two issues you feel are the most pressing, and those may be the reason you picked up this book in the first place.

Common Shifts

In the previous chapter, I briefly mentioned six areas people most commonly ask about because they are the most pressing issues in their lives. In general, changes people would like to make often fall into these categories. The following questionnaire can help you zero in on each category to determine your most pressing issues. After completing the questionnaire, pick one or two of the issues that feel the most important to you and start there in your crystal work.

Life Energy Questionnaire

So that you can do regular check-ins with yourself, I recommend that you take out a sheet of paper, or your journal, and rate your experience as follows. Or you can download a copy of this questionnaire at http://newharbinger.com/32952 and fill it out whenever inspired. For the questions below, please check all that apply.

Health and Wellness

1. I am unhappy with my current state of physical health. _____

2. I have chronic health issues that I have been unable to resolve. _____

3. Doctors have been unable to diagnose my health issues. _____

4. I have more than three areas of health I feel need improvement. _____

5. My health issues moderately to significantly affect my quality of life. _____

6. I am unhappy with my current state of mental or emotional health. _____

7. I have more than one mental or emotional health issue. _____

8. I rate the level of my mental or emotional health issues as moderate to severe. _____

9. My mental and emotional health issues significantly affect my quality of life. _____

10. I take medication to help control my emotional health. _____

Total checked = _____

Prosperity and Abundance

1. I am dissatisfied with my current financial situation. _____

2. I never seem to have enough money. _____

3. My finances fluctuate wildly. _____

4. I have a poor attitude about my finances. _____

5. My poor financial situation moderately to significantly affects the quality of my life. _____

Total checked x 2 = _____

Purpose (Career and Life)

1. I don't have a sense of purpose in my career or life. _____

2. I feel dissatisfied all the time. _____

3. I dread or dislike going to work each day. _____

4. I come home from work deflated and exhausted. _____

5. I hate my work. _____

6. I feel unfulfilled by my work. _____

7. Outside of my work, my life feels purposeless. _____

8. I don't feel creatively or intellectually fulfilled in my life. _____

9. I don't engage in any activities that provide me with a strong sense of purpose. _____

10. My whole life feels like a grind. _____

Total checked = _____

Self-Love and Self-Esteem

1. I have poor self-esteem. _____

2. I have difficulty listing five things I like about myself. _____

3. I can easily list five things I dislike about myself. _____

4. I always worry people don't like me or will find me annoying. _____

5. My self-esteem issues have a moderate to severe effect on the quality of my life. _____

Total checked x 2 = _____

Forgiveness

1. I am carrying anger or bitterness toward people in my life. _____

2. I carry anger or bitterness toward myself for things I have done or decisions I have made. _____

3. I know I need to forgive others, but I find it difficult to let go of the anger. _____

4. I know I need to forgive myself, but I find it difficult to let go of the anger. _____

5. My inability to forgive has a moderate to severe effect on the quality of my life. _____

Total checked x 2 = _____

1. I feel unfulfilled in my romantic partnership. _____

2. I am lonely. _____

3. I am unhappy with my current relationship status. _____

4. I wish I had more friends. _____

5. I am unhappy with my family relationships. _____

6. I am dissatisfied with my work relationships. _____

7. I know all of my relationships need work. _____

8. I wish I had more of a social life. _____

9. I don't really belong to many social groups. _____

10. I spend most of my time alone, and I wish I didn't. _____

Total checked = _____

WHAT IT ALL MEANS

The areas with the highest scores indicate your strongest areas of priority currently or the places where you have the least satisfaction in your life that could use the most immediate energy healing.

Aligning Your Desired Shift with the Right Crystal

In the previous chapter, I identified a process for selecting a crystal based on lattice system, color, opacity, shape, and type. You can use this process to select a crystal to help you deal with the issues you've selected. After determining the key issues you want to work with, ask yourself the following:

- What are the primary colors and chakras associated with this issue? Select the color based on this answer. For example, if your primary issue is prosperity, then green crystals may be your best choice. If it is self-esteem, then yellow crystals would be a better choice.

- How do I want to affect the energy? Select your lattice structure based on your answer using the handy reference chart below.

I want to…	Lattice Structure
protect	monoclinic
expand	monoclinic
grow	monoclinic
repel unwanted energy	triclinic
contain energy or stop energy loss	triclinic
balance energies	triclinic
correct spiritual, emotional, mental, or physical imbalances	triclinic
remove blockages of all types	orthorhombic

I want to...	Lattice Structure
undo an old habit	orthorhombic
clear energy	orthorhombic
cleanse energy	orthorhombic
get unstuck	orthorhombic
get rid of energy that no longer serves me	orthorhombic
attract energy	tetragonal
change negative energy to positive	tetragonal
amplify positive energy	tetragonal
attract something new	tetragonal
manifest something	hexagonal
increase energy (in general)	hexagonal
increase physical, emotional, or energetic vitality	hexagonal
meet goals more quickly	hexagonal
amplify an energy that is already present	hexagonal
set intention	hexagonal
increase the power of intention, affirmation, or visualization	hexagonal
improve physical health	cubic

I want to…	Lattice Structure
stabilize some type of energy (emotional, spiritual, physical)	cubic
experience grounding	cubic

- Is this an issue of too much energy flow or not enough energy flow? If too much, such as an overabundance of self-confidence, then select an opaque crystal; if not enough, such as poor self-esteem, select a transparent crystal.

Intuitive Selection

Another way to select crystals for each of your issues is intuitively. If you consider yourself an intuitive person, then this may work well for you.

I often wind up setting an intention for a crystal when I go shopping without realizing I'm doing so. For example, in recent weeks, I've been focusing on cleansing and clearing my home and life. I've been working on getting rid of things that don't serve me so as I move forward, I can bring more of the energy I desire into my life. One day a few weeks ago as I was sorting through a closet, my husband came in and asked if I wanted to go for a drive since it was a nice day. I happily left my closet and headed for the car.

As we frequently do when we leave the house without a destination in mind, Jim and I wound up in a crystal shop. In the store, I was immediately drawn to a large cluster of clear quartz with beautiful green embedded in the points. I'd never seen anything quite like it, but I knew I had to have it. The crystal came home with me. On our way home, I picked up the mail, and in it was a crystal subscription box that had a small piece of the same quartz I'd just purchased.

Doing some research when I got home, I discovered both pieces were quartz with chlorite inclusions, or flaws. What's interesting about chlorite is it's the perfect crystal for cleansing and clearing old energy to make way for new energy. It was the perfect crystal for what my current goals were, and twice in a three-hour period, it came into my life to help support my intention. The crystals had chosen me.

To select crystals intuitively, do the following:

1. Determine which issues you'll be working with. Take a few moments before crystal shopping to close your eyes, breathe deeply, and focus on those issues.

2. Set your intention: "I will find the perfect crystals to help me shift the energy of _____." Do this before you leave to go shopping and then again just before you enter the crystal shop.

3. Then, with your intention in mind, start to shop. Pay attention and go where you are drawn. If a crystal calls your attention, go to it.

4. Hold the crystal in your nondominant hand, which is your receiving hand (so your right hand if you are left-handed, or your left hand if you are right-handed). Close your eyes and restate your intention for the crystal. Notice how the crystal feels in your hand.

5. You'll learn to discern when you are getting the signal that you are holding the right crystal for you. For me, it feels like something clicks into place—a feeling of relief and satisfaction, as well as a comfortable sensation in the hand that is holding the

crystal. Others may see images in their mind or just "know" that it is the right crystal.

I call this "letting the crystal choose you." If you are drawn to a certain crystal, or if that crystal appears repeatedly in your life, there's a good chance you need that energy. The crystal is choosing you, and if it is meant to be yours, it will be.

Where to Find Crystals

Crystals are growing in popularity; many people are instinctively drawn to them for their beauty, not realizing the beneficial energy they bring. With such an abundance in availability in these treasures from the planet, there are more places than ever where you can find them.

ROCK SHOPS (CRYSTAL, WICCA, AND METAPHYSICAL STORES)

Many places have stores dedicated to selling crystals, and these are usually a great place to start. Rock, Wicca, and metaphysical shops often have employees and owners who are passionate about crystals and are excited to help customers find the perfect gem to meet their needs.

GEM FAIRS

Gem fairs travel from location to location around the country (often fairgrounds) and have dozens of vendors offering great deals on all types of crystals, minerals, and gems. There's usually a nominal fee to get in, but the treasures you'll find at these shows are pretty cool, often with many unusual specimens, and the prices tend to be affordable.

ROCK AND MINERAL SHOWS

Many towns and counties have mineral hobby groups that put on local mineral shows where gems are for sale. These are usually annual events, and they may range from a few vendors to a dozen or more.

Mineral shows are often held at county fairgrounds, and they cost a small fee to get in. However, you'll find passionate hobbyists with interesting specimens you may not be able to find elsewhere. Take cash. While many of the vendors accept credit and debit cards, you may be able to negotiate better deals if you're carrying cash.

CRAFT SHOWS

Craft shows and bazaars are also an excellent source of handmade crystal jewelry. These pieces are usually one-of-a-kind originals. While vendors do sometimes accept credit cards, take cash and you may get a better deal.

METAPHYSICAL FAIRS

I've never been to a metaphysical fair where there isn't at least one person vending crystal specimens and another vending handmade crystal jewelry. Metaphysical fairs may have a small entry fee, but they are a great place to score crystals.

HOME STORES

This one seemed odd to me at first, but I find a lot of crystals in home stores. For some of my favorites, see the resources section. The crystals you'll find there are pretty common (there's a lot of amethyst, quartz, and rose quartz), but it's a good place for an inexpensive specimen. Some people worry the crystals they find here might be fake—that is, synthetic. I haven't found this to be the case. However, if the crystal appears too perfect (without flaws, extremely even in color and shape), chances are it is man-made.

ROCK HOUNDING

If you're an adventurer, you can head out to go rock hounding. Rock hounds search for crystals in nature; you can find many websites with maps that show you locations where you can hunt for crystals yourself. There's a cost for equipment and possibly entry to certain lands and parks, but after that, the crystals are free if you're willing to work for them. Double-check before you go to make sure you're not trespassing and can remove specimens from the location you choose.

ONLINE

There are many sources of crystals online. You can find auctions on eBay, sellers on Etsy, and numerous crystal and mineral online dealers. You can also try one of the many crystal subscription crates (see "Resources"). The only drawback of online crystals is you won't be able to hold them to feel their energy, but it is my belief that if a crystal is meant to be yours, it will come to you any way it can—even from online sources. Check seller ratings on auction sites and double-check with sources like the Better Business Bureau for the reputation of companies you purchase crystals from so you don't get ripped off.

Crystals Come and Go as You Need Them

When I started with crystals, I brought a few home. Then I brought more, and then more. My crystal collection has grown and shifted. It is a living organism with a mind of its own. I believe crystals come to you when you need them, they stay as long as you need them, and if you no longer need them, you may be guided to give them away (or they might just disappear). Sometimes a crystal will come to you for a reason; it's something you need. When you don't need it anymore, you may be called to give it away, or you may lose it. I've had this happen more than once. Some crystals come to you for a lifetime. These are the crystals that are treasured keepsakes you love and care for throughout your entire life.

In the early days of my adult crystal collection, I had a small pouch of crystals I kept with me always. I thought I needed that pouch for protection because I felt so vulnerable and exposed when I went out in the world. One day I was getting ready to go somewhere, and I had my pouch of crystals with me. I set them down on the counter, turned around to do something on another counter, and turned back around less than 10 seconds later. The pouch was gone. I searched high and low; I practically tore my house apart but couldn't find the pouch even though it had disappeared in less than 10 seconds. I had no choice but to journey into the world without my crystals, and I discovered I was just fine without them. My early feelings of vulnerability had gone away sometime during my crystal work, but I relied so much on the crystals that I didn't realize I no longer needed them. That was a valuable lesson for me.

Years later, the crystals from that pouch started appearing one at a time in various locations in my house. Once I no longer relied on them, they found their way back to me, and as I found them, I was called to give them away one at a time to others who needed their energy.

Aligning with crystals is an individual process. Love the crystals you have while you have them, but never grow so attached that you rely on them. They will serve you well when you need the energy they provide as long as you select them with the intention to bring positive vibration into your life and are willing to let go if that energy no longer serves you.

CHAPTER 8

Crystal Safety

In their enthusiasm for crystals, many people don't realize there are safety concerns. For example, you'll find many people who recommend ingesting crystals in some way (usually in the form of gem-infused water, also known as a crystal elixir). So it's important when handling crystals or ingesting elixirs to take appropriate safety precautions.

Crystal Toxicity Chart

While it is unlikely that your crystals will poison you, it is important to understand that crystals are made up of elements that could be harmful if you ingested them or failed to use proper care.

The following is a list of ingredients that are poisonous to humans and pets and the crystals that contain them. Never put these crystals directly in water you will drink or bathe in; keep them away from food, children, and pets; and use caution when handling them.

Aluminum

- ajoite
- alexandrite
- aquamarine
- beryls
- dumortierite
- emerald
- garnet
- iolite
- Kansas Pop Rocks (Boji Stones)
- kunzite
- labradorite
- lepidolite
- moldavite
- moonstone
- morganite
- prehnite
- ruby
- sapphire
- sodalite
- spinel
- staurolite
- stilbite
- sugilite
- sunstone
- tanzanite
- topaz
- tourmaline
- turquoise
- variscite
- vesuvianite
- wavelite
- zoisite

Sulfur

- Boji Stones
- markasite
- peacock stones
- pyrite
- sovellite

Copper

- adamite
- amazonite
- azurite
- bronchantite
- cavansite
- chalcantite
- chalcopyrite (peacock stone)
- chrysocolla
- copper
- covellite
- cuprite
- dioptase
- malachite
- mohawkite
- silica
- smithsonite
- turquoise

Arsenic

- adamite
- mohawkite
- realgar

Lead

- galena
- stibnite
- wulfenite

Asbestos (unpolished crystals only)

- actinolite
- pietersite
- serpentine
- tigers eye
- tremolite

Fluorine

- fluorite

Strontium

- celestite

Mercury

- cinnabar

- torbenite

- treated and artificially colored gemstones

- zircon

Wash Your Hands

The biggest safety tip I can offer you is something simple you learned when you were a child, and it's a practice you engage in multiple times a day: wash your hands. After you handle crystals, it's always best to wash your hands to remove any substances that may have leached from your crystals and onto your hands. Likewise, wipe down any surface the crystals have been on, especially if it's an eating or food-preparation surface. Again, I don't want to panic you, but I do want to urge you to exercise due caution so you don't experience unintended consequences in your enthusiasm for crystals.

Crystal Elixir Safety

I'll start by saying I'm not a huge fan of recommending gem-infused elixirs to people who don't know a lot about crystals primarily because of the safety issues associated with them; most people don't realize you can't just toss any crystal in water and safely consume it. Some people hear that you can drink a crystal elixir and proceed without much research, pouring water over any crystal they find and then drinking the water. This is not without risks.

Many crystals contain unsafe substances that you don't want to ingest, such as asbestos, aluminum, arsenic, and strontium. While I don't want you to panic and think your crystals will poison you, for the sake of your physical health, you probably don't want to randomly drop a crystal in a glass of water before you drink or use the water, on the off chance it will leech poisonous substances into the water.

If you do decide you'd like to try crystal elixirs, please study the chart above carefully and research any crystals you plan to use in an elixir if you decide you want to put the crystals directly in the water. In the next chapter, I offer a method for making safe elixirs with any crystal.

Crystal Safety for Children and Pets

When my now college-aged sons were babies and toddlers, they would put virtually anything in their mouth. Now they are adults, and it's up to them to monitor the safety of what they consume, but I remember the days of little grabbing hands, having everything on high shelves, and monitoring what the kids picked up and put in their mouth.

Because they are colorful and often small, crystals can look like candy treats to young children. Store these crystals out of reach of young hands and teach your children that they are rocks and not candy. Only allow your children to have access to your crystals when you are nearby and watching closely, and teach them to look but not touch. If your children do touch your crystals, teach them that they always need to wash their hands after handling them and that they should never put their hands or fingers in their mouth (or crystals for that matter) until they've washed them.

You know your pets, and you're most likely aware of which pets have a propensity to eat (or lick) first and ask questions later. I recommend using extreme caution around these pets but exercising care with all pets and young children since they can be unpredictable.

For pet safety, store crystals (especially smaller specimens) in containers where they can't be reached or where the container is sealed so your pet can't get into them. When your crystals are out, keep a close eye on pets or use them in a space where your pets can't get to them.

Simple Safety Rules

Although crystals contain some toxic substances, there is no need to be afraid of them. Keep them out of reach of kids and pets, don't submerse them directly in water (or other liquids) and drink it, wash your hands after handling them, and wipe up any surfaces that double as places where you work with crystals and eat food. Other than that, as long as you're not throwing them at windows or other people, you shouldn't have a lot of safety concerns when working with your crystals. And, with the appropriate precautions, crystal elixirs can be a powerful way to spread the energy of your crystals throughout your living and working spaces and your life.

CHAPTER 9

Making and Using Crystal Elixirs

Crystal elixirs, when safely made, can spread the energy of the crystals quickly. The water holds the vibration of the crystals, so any elixir infused with the essence of crystals offers another opportunity to change the vibrational frequency of places, physiology, or situations.

Safe Crystal Elixir Method

Crystals placed in proximity to water can infuse the water with their vibration. Many people make elixirs by dropping a crystal in the water, but I prefer the safer method that follows. Due to the proximity of the crystals to the water, the vibration of the water will start to match that of the crystals via entrainment.

Safe Crystal Elixir

Materials:

- Large, clean glass jar with a clean lid to seal it

- Potable water

- Larger container (such as a box or bowl) big enough to hold the sealed jar

- 4 or 5 crystals

Instructions:

1. Fill the jar with clean water and seal it with a clean lid.

2. Place the jar in the larger container and surround it with the crystals, allowing the crystals to touch the outside of the jar.

3. Infuse for 24 hours.

Using the Elixir

The properties of the crystal infuse the elixir. Therefore, you use a crystal elixir made with a single crystal for the same issues you use that crystal in other ways. For example, if insomnia is an issue, then a few drops of amethyst-infused elixir in bathwater or in a small glass of water before bedtime may promote restful sleep just as an amethyst on the bedside table does the same.

DRINK IT

Use four drops of a chosen crystal elixir in eight ounces of water and drink it daily until the energy of a situation has shifted. For example, if you are feeling creatively blocked, you can make an aragonite crystal elixir. Then, add four drops of the crystal elixir to eight ounces of water and drink it twice a day while setting your intention for creativity.

SPRAY IT

Add crystal elixir to an aromatherapy spray (about four drops per eight ounces). For example, for better sleep, you can infuse water with amethyst and add four drops of the amethyst elixir to a sleep-inducing pillow spray that has seven ounces of water, one ounce of vodka, eight drops of lavender essential oil, and eight drops of chamomile essential oil. Spray it on your pillow nightly. Amethyst is known to be good for insomnia and to induce guidance dreams.

You can also add two or three drops of a crystal elixir to four ounces of water and use it to mist plants. Moss agate is a good gardener's stone with earth and plant energy.

Another good elixir spray is what I call "juju spray," which is any spray I spritz around my home and workspaces to shift the energy of a situation. For example, my favorite juju spray to turn negative energy into positive contains eight ounces of water, one teaspoon of Himalayan pink salt, four drops of smoky quartz crystal elixir, and two drops each of grapefruit essential oil, lemon essential oil, orange essential oil, and ginger essential oil.

BATHE IN IT

Add one ounce of a crystal elixir to your bathwater and bathe in it. If you bathe before bedtime, you'll want to use different crystal elixirs than if you bathe to start your day so you can use an elixir with the appropriate energy. For example, you wouldn't want to use a stimulating crystal elixir made from garnet at bedtime, but it would be fantastic to start your day. Likewise, you wouldn't want to use a calming crystal elixir made from blue lace agate first thing in the morning, but it's fantastic at bedtime.

I also like to use crystal elixirs in baths for spiritual and emotional cleansing. For example, every full moon, I add to my bathwater one ounce of rose quartz and clear quartz–infused water for unconditional love and purification, two tablespoons of Himalayan pink salt to cleanse energy, and six drops each of rosemary and lavender essential oils for peace. I soak for 10 minutes and then allow the water to drain completely to wash away any negativity before I step out of the tub and dry off.

WASH AND CLEAN WITH IT

Crystal elixirs can cleanse energy while cleaning products clean you or your home. I like to mix four drops of crystal elixir into my beauty products, like shampoo and body wash. I vary which elixir I use based on what I'm trying to do with the energy. For example, if I need to be creative, I might use an aragonite-infused elixir in my morning shampoo, and if I want to have dreams that allow me to communicate with my higher self, I might add a labradorite-infused elixir to my evening body wash.

I also add elixirs to my cleaning products. My favorite cleaning product is a home steamer that cleans surfaces with hot steam instead of chemical products. I enjoy adding a few drops of essential oil for scent and a crystal elixir made from chlorite phantom quartz, which is a cleansing crystal, to the steamer before I steam my surfaces.

Getting Started with Crystal Elixirs

We live in a society where people sometimes believe if a little is good, more is better. However, remember that crystal elixirs contain the same powerful energy as the crystals themselves. Therefore, you may want to start with moderation to determine how energy shifts will affect you when using the elixirs. I suggest starting with a single daily practice of using a crystal elixir, such as consuming the four drops in eight ounces of water daily, and then add other uses after you know how it affects you. Likewise, start with a single crystal elixir focused on one of the areas you've identified where you'd like to shift the energy, and then add more as the first practice becomes an established habit.

CHAPTER 10

Caring for and Maintaining Your Crystals

While crystals are pretty low maintenance, caring for them properly can help them maintain the highest vibrational energy possible, which is essential if you want them to function at peak capacity as you use them.

Crystals have a pure vibration, but just as crystal vibration affects you and your environment, so does your energy—as well as energy from other people, situations, emotions, and places—affect your crystals. If you recall from earlier chapters, I mentioned that when two bodies oscillating at different frequencies maintain proximity to each other, they lock into phase, or entrain, just like metronomes or pendulum clocks do. So while crystal vibrations are affecting you, you're also affecting the vibration of the crystals. I find that eventually, you and your crystals meet somewhere in the middle, with your vibration raising to match the crystals and their vibration lowering to match yours.

Therefore, if you want your crystals to continue to work for you and help you raise your vibration to their level, you need to maintain them via cleansing. This is not simply washing dirt and dust off crystals. Instead, you are cleansing their energy so they return to their original high vibration. And you, having been working with the crystals, are vibrating at the new higher level. With both your new higher vibration and the renewed high vibration from the cleansed crystals, you meet in the middle again through entrainment, this time at an even higher level than previously. Thus, you continue a cycle of cleansing and vibrating slightly higher yourself each time you cleanse a crystal.

Cleansing When You First Bring Your Crystal Home

When you bring a crystal home for the first time, it's new to you, but it certainly isn't new. While you may know where you picked up the crystal, you have no idea where that crystal has been over the past few million years. Chances are, it has entrained to the energy of wherever it has been, whether in homes, shops, or the land, and it isn't currently vibrating at optimal frequency—even if a friend has gifted it to you. So, when that crystal comes home with you, the very first thing you should always do is cleanse it using any of the methods I outline in this chapter. This restores the crystal to its original high vibration and removes any stuck energy from where it has been that may have lowered its vibration.

A Schedule for Cleansing Crystals

While I always recommend listening to your intuition and cleansing crystals whenever you feel they need it, I also suggest following a regular schedule for crystal cleansing so you don't forget to do so.

DAILY

For crystals in heavy use—those that you wear or use daily in some way—I recommend daily cleansing first thing in the morning to make sure they always vibrate at the highest possible level for you. If you are going through a period with heavy energy, such as a major life change like a divorce, death in the family, or loss of a job, I also recommend daily cleansing for any crystals in your environment, especially those that absorb negative energy, like black tourmaline and hematite.

WEEKLY

For crystals you use a few times a week, weekly cleansing is usually sufficient unless you are going through a difficult time, as noted in the previous section. I recommend starting your week (either Sunday morning or Sunday evening) with a ritual cleansing of these crystals so you start off your week on a positive note.

MONTHLY

All of your crystals need to be cleansed at least monthly. I recommend doing it every full moon; I liken this to changing your smoke detector batteries on Labor Day and Memorial Day. Doing it every full moon is an effective way to remember monthly cleansing. The full moon may also be appropriate for cleansing because of its energetic properties. Many schools of thought, including astrology, believe that when the moon is full, it has a special and powerful energy that can bring about positive change. Therefore, many crystal practitioners use this full moon energy every month to cleanse their crystals and charge them with positivity.

Crystal Cleansing Methods

As I pointed out earlier, cleansing doesn't mean washing your crystals. It means removing any energies that have collected from use and environment and returning them to their original vibrational frequency. There are many methods you can use to cleanse your crystals; how you choose to do it is up to you. I use a variety of methods depending on what's available, what I feel intuitively called to do, or what I feel like doing at that moment.

People often suggest cleansing crystals using salt and water, but it's not a method I recommend. While this method can be effective, there are some crystals that become damaged when exposed to salt, water, or saltwater. Therefore, I skip recommending this because there are so many other effective methods with less risk of inadvertently damaging crystals.

MOONLIGHT OR SUNLIGHT

One popular way of cleansing large volumes of crystals is to leave them out overnight in the moonlight or for several hours during the day in sunlight. Contrary to popular belief, you don't need light from a full moon, but you do need a noticeable amount of moonlight. So this isn't an effective method for cloudy days or nights, or for nights when there is a new or crescent moon. Leave the crystals in the light for six hours or longer for cleansing.

SOUND

I'm a sound healing practitioner and musician, so sound is one of my favorite ways of cleansing crystals. You can use a singing bowl, a tuning fork, tingshas (which are Tibetan chimes), wind chimes, a gong, small hand chimes, or anything else that produces a clear, ringing tone. Gather the crystals you want to cleanse in one location and, sitting as close to the crystals as you can, allow your instrument to ring. Keep sounding the instrument for one to three minutes for best results.

SMOKE FROM BURNING HERBS, WOODS, RESINS, AND INCENSE

Smoke is another effective crystal cleanser. There are many herbs, resins, and woods that produce cleansing smoke, including:

- sage
- palo santo
- sweetgrass
- frankincense
- cedar
- lavender

To use this method, gather the crystals you wish to cleanse into a bowl. Light your herb, resin, wood, or incense and allow it to flame until it begins to smolder. Blow out the flame and direct the smoke from the smoldering piece into your bowl full of crystals, stirring the crystals around so they are all exposed to the smoke. Alternatively, lay all your crystals out on a surface and direct the smoke over them.

HANDS-ON ENERGY HEALING

If you practice a hands-on energy healing technique such as Reiki, Quantum Touch, Healing Touch, Matrix Energetics, or similar, you can also use this energy to cleanse crystals. Hold the crystals in your hands and direct the cleansing energy to flow through your hands and into the crystals for about three minutes. Since I am a Reiki master, this is typically how I cleanse my crystals when I bring them home. I cleanse them in my hands in the car on the way home so that when they enter my environment, the energy is bright and new.

CRYSTALS WITH CLEANSING EFFECTS

You may also see other crystal practitioners who suggest some crystals are self-cleansing, such as citrine, and you can use certain crystals with this quality to cleanse the rest. Even if crystals are used to cleanse others or are listed as self-cleansing, I recommend cleansing them regularly to return them to their highest vibration.

You can use clusters of clear quartz to cleanse smaller crystals. Place the smaller crystals into a large bed of freshly cleansed clear quartz and allow them to sit there for about six hours for maximum cleansing benefits.

You can also use freshly cleansed selenite to cleanse other crystals. Place the crystals you want to cleanse in a bowl or zipper bag with the freshly cleansed selenite for about six hours.

Other Maintenance

There are a few other things you'll want to do as regular crystal maintenance.

- Dust crystals every few days to remove any dust or debris.

- Wipe crystals you wear with a soft damp cloth to remove body oil, dust, and debris. If crystal jewelry will stand up to deeper cleaning, many crystal or jewelry shops will return your pieces to their bright, sparkly condition if you ask them to.

- If you carry a black stone, like black tourmaline or hematite for protection, and it breaks, it means it has absorbed as much negative energy as it can. Express gratitude, return it to the earth (bury it or place it in a garden for instance), and replace it.

Crystals for a Lifetime

That's really all you need to do to maintain your crystals. Cleanse them energetically when you bring them home and on a schedule depending on how much you use them. Also keep them physically clean. Doing this allows your crystals to continue to vibrate at their optimal frequency so they have clear energy when you begin to direct their energy in your life.

PART 3

WAYS TO DIRECT THE ENERGY OF CRYSTALS

CHAPTER 11

Placing Crystals in Strategic Locations

I have crystals all over my house. Some are placed strategically, and others are placed where I think they're pretty or shown to their best effect. And while I think both methods of crystal placement are perfectly fine, strategic placement of the appropriate crystals can have a huge effect on the energies that manifest in your life and spaces.

For example, I have sprinkled the perimeter of my property and the outer perimeter of my home with small smoky quartz chips. The reason I did this was so that all energy crossing onto my property and crossing into my home is transmuted into positive energy in order to positively affect my living and working spaces, family, plants, and pets. I have done this for others as well. I also have prosperity crystals in my home's wealth area; sleep crystals (mostly amethyst) and protection crystals in my bedroom for better sleep, dreams, and protection while I sleep; and crystals that stimulate creativity in my workspace, in my music area, and in the career and creativity areas of my home.

How do I know how to do this? I use a combination of the principles of fêng shui, intuition, and placement of crystals that support the activities that occur in certain living and work spaces.

Fêng Shui Bagua

Fêng shui is a Chinese system of decoration, placement, and organization that determines the placement of furniture, decorations, objects, and colors to promote optimal function of life force energy.

The primary tool in fêng shui is called the "bagua." The bagua is a chart or map designating areas in spaces that promote certain energies, such as prosperity, family, spirituality, or career. The bagua designates either eight or nine sectors depending on the school of fêng shui you follow.

There are many schools of fêng shui, but the two you're most likely to find are traditional fêng shui and Western (or black hat) fêng shui.

- In traditional fêng shui, the areas of the bagua are based on compass directions.

- In Western or black hat fêng shui, the areas of the bagua are based on the location of the front door facing into the space.

Both traditional and black hat fêng shui use similar baguas, but how you determine the various areas of your home will depend on which method you choose. I don't specifically recommend one type or the other, but I do recommend you choose only one of these schools and place crystals according to either the traditional or the Western school instead of using a mishmash of both so you don't send confusing information to the universe. Be clear on which you wish to use, and stick with that. In my house, I use traditional fêng shui, which is based on compass directions, for placement.

Below is a representation of the bauga used for both schools of fêng shui. This chart is itself a compass. For Western fêng shui, align your front door with the bottom center of the chart.

Wealth and Prosperity	Fame and Recognition	Love, Marriage, and Relationships
Traditional: Southeast	Traditional: South	Traditional: Southwest
Western: Back left	Western: Back center	Western: Back right
Family and Community	Health and Well-Being	Children, Creativity, and Communication
Traditional: Southwest or center	Traditional: East	Traditional: West
Western: Center left	Western: Center	Western: Center right
Knowledge, Self-Cultivation, and Spirituality	Career, Success at Work, and Life Journey	Helpful People, Benefactors, and Travel
Traditional: Northeast	Traditional: North	Traditional: Northwest
Western: Front left	Western: Front center	Western: Front right

WEALTH AND PROSPERITY AREA

In traditional fêng shui, the bauga shows the wealth and prosperity area in the southeast corner of a home, room, or space. In Western fêng shui, it is in the back left corner. Its element is wood, and the colors are brown, green, purple, gold, and blue. Crystals to place in this area of a home, workspace, or room include crystals in the colors indicated above, as well as crystals that support wealth and prosperity. Some crystals to place in your prosperity sector to support wealth and abundance include:

- amazonite
- ametrine
- citrine

- green or blue apatite
- green aventurine
- pyrite

Some items you can place in your prosperity sector include natural citrine points, an abundance goddess holding a green crystal, and a fêng shui crystal money tree with citrine or green crystals.

FAME AND RECOGNITION AREA

In traditional fêng shui, the fame and recognition area sits in the south of your home, room, or workspace. In Western fêng shui, it is the back center. Its element is fire, and associated colors are shades of red (including pinks). Therefore, if you wish to promote recognition or fame in any area of your life, place crystals in this sector that are red in color, or those that support fame and recognition:

- garnet
- red carnelian
- red hematite

- ruby
- spinel

In your fame or recognition area, consider placing cherry quartz, which is a manufactured red quartz believed to have metaphysical properties and hang a garnet pendant from a window or hook.

LOVE, MARRIAGE, AND RELATIONSHIPS AREA

In traditional fêng shui, the area that supports love and relationships (and also family life) is in the southwest sector of your home, room, or workspace. In Western fêng shui, it sits at the back right of any of those locations. The element associated with this area is earth, and the colors are pink, red, and white. Crystals in these colors, as well as other crystals that improve love and relationships, in this location can strengthen love relationships. Other stones that will fit the bill in this area include:

- emerald
- kunzite
- morganite
- pink tourmaline
- ruby

I love that the kitchen, which is the center of my family life because it is where we've always spent so much time together, is in my home's family sector. Wherever it is in your home, try placing rose quartz in this area, as well as a piece of unakite, which is a green and pink stone supporting all types of love energy. Spray a homemade emerald-infused elixir made with water, emerald, and rose otto essential oil here, and keep a small cellar of pink Himalayan salt, which is derived from pink halite crystals, in the area.

FAMILY AND COMMUNITY AREA

Traditional fêng shui's bagua doesn't specify a family area of your home, room, or workspace. Instead, it's incorporated into relationships in the southwest or children in the west. In Western fêng shui, it's in the center left sector. This is an important area for keeping family and community ties strong and healthy. Its element is wood, and its associated colors are greens and blues. Therefore, crystals in these colors are beneficial in this area. They include:

- blue lace agate
- emerald
- iolite

- lapis lazuli
- malachite
- sodalite

If you are following the traditional bagua, you can still support this energy by placing crystals in locations in your home where friends and family gather to cultivate community. I do this primarily in my living room and studio space. For example, in your living room, place an emerald in the southwest sector, or place a blue lace agate in office spaces or places where you receive guests.

HEALTH AND WELL-BEING AREA

In traditional fêng shui, this important area is located in the east, while in Western fêng shui, it's located in the center of any space because it is so vital to balance of the whole. Its element is earth, and the associated colors are brown, yellow, and orange. Crystals in these colors, along with crystals supporting specific health conditions, are beneficial here and include:

- aragonite
- carnelian
- jasper
- smoky quartz
- tigers eye

This is a great place for a small shelf of crystals that support various health concerns for family members. You can also place on the shelf a large piece of carnelian or smoky quartz to support general health. My shelf in this sector holds crystals that support my autoimmune disease, Hashimoto's thyroiditis, and my husband's heart disease. Since autoimmune diseases are associated with the root and crown chakras, I have red and white crystals here, as well as green crystals for my husband's heart health. I also have aquamarine in quartz on this shelf to balance my throat chakra, which provides thyroid support.

I love the idea of placing a small shelf in this area so you can place various crystals to support any health conditions your family members may have. Place each with intention for optimal health for the family member it supports.

CHILDREN, CREATIVITY, AND COMMUNICATION AREA

In traditional fêng shui, this area is located in the western part of your home, room, or workspace. In Western fêng shui, it sits in the center right of any of these spaces. It is associated with the element of metal, and colors include yellow, white, silver, gray, and copper. Therefore, crystals in these colors placed in this location are excellent to boost creativity, improve communication, and nurture your children. You can also choose crystals that support creativity to place here. Some crystals that meet either of these criteria include:

- aragonite
- carnelian
- citrine

- copper
- galena
- sodalite

Try placing aragonite and a piece of sodalite in this sector to enhance creativity. If your front door is in the western sector, place a carnelian tower nearby so the first thing new energy entering your home sweeps past is something that nurtures creativity. This will bring more creative energy into your home every time the door opens.

KNOWLEDGE, SELF-CULTIVATION, AND SPIRITUALITY AREA

In traditional fêng shui, this area is located in the northeast of your home, workspace, or room. In Western fêng shui, it is front right. It is associated with the element of earth, and its colors are black, blue, and green. Therefore, crystals in these colors as well as crystals that support knowledge and spirituality are beneficial when placed here. These include:

- amethyst
- black tourmaline
- hematite
- lapis lazuli
- malachite
- turquoise

I have an L-shaped house, so this sector is absent in my home. Homes with unusual shapes often have an absent sector, since the bagua is based on the home having a square or rectangular footprint. However, you can remedy these absent spaces by creating an outdoor "room." To do this, determine where the farthest corner of the missing room would be, and place the element associated with the missing sector in that corner. In my house, I created this space by placing a small piece of amethyst where the northeast corner of the house would be to create an outdoor "corner" to my home in order to ensure I continue to strengthen this area of my life. When I cleanse my home with sound or smudge it, I always walk the perimeter of this "room" to energetically define it. You can also create a perimeter to the "room" by sprinkling crystal chips along the general outline of the missing space or spritzing a crystal elixir in the appropriate element for the missing sector.

CAREER, SUCCESS AT WORK, AND LIFE JOURNEY AREA

In traditional fêng shui, this sector sits in the north area of your home, workspace, or room. In Western fêng shui, it is front and center. Its element is water, and the colors are black, dark blue, dark green, and gray. Therefore, placing crystals in these colors, as well as crystals that promote success, are appropriate in this area. These include:

- citrine
- iolite
- malachite
- obsidian
- tigers eye

My bedroom is in the north sector of my home, which isn't super conducive to work and career. However, I do have a citrine point in my bedroom closet, which is the northernmost part of the house. In order to make up for an inauspicious location for a bedroom, I've arranged my work and studio spaces to enhance this area. To that end, I keep tigers eye in the northern sector of my workspace and an iolite and sunstone sphere in the north sector of my studio.

HELPFUL PEOPLE, BENEFACTORS, AND TRAVEL AREA

In traditional fêng shui, this area is in the northwest of any space, home, or room. In Western fêng shui, it sits at the front right. The element is metal, and the colors are gray, white, and black. Therefore, stones in these colors work well in this location, as do any stones that promote travel. Some stones to consider placing here include:

- black tourmaline
- hematite
- malachite
- snowflake obsidian
- turquoise

I have a perpetual case of wanderlust, so travel is important to me, especially since my kids are older and out of the house now. Unfortunately, my husband's rather chaotic office is in the northwest corner for our home, and I don't go in there a lot. However, I have placed a piece of hematite in there on a windowsill. To make up for the fact my home's travel sector is in my husband's domain, I've enhanced it in other spaces where I spend a lot of time. For instance, I have a lovely piece of malachite in the northwest sector of my main workspace, and a piece of snowflake obsidian sphere in my upstairs studio and meditation space. If travel is important to you, try some of the above strategies to help enhance the energy in your home.

Placement by Activity

You can also place crystals around the home to support the activities you pursue in each location. So the crystals you will have in your kitchen will be different than those in your bedroom, bathroom, or workspaces because you have different intentions when you use each of these rooms.

WORKSPACES

If you have a dedicated office space, consider the activity you do there. For example, in my workspace, I do my writing, pay bills, do my taxes, work on my computer, and engage in other business activities. Therefore, I place crystals that support these activities, which means I choose crystals for work success, financial abundance, creativity, and communication, and to absorb negative energy that sometimes accompanies work.

To determine which crystals you need in your workspace, make a list of the activities you perform there as well as your intentions for the space. Then, choose crystals based on color, lattice type, and the other criteria that support those activities.

FAMILY AND COMMUNITY SPACES

Family and community spaces might include your living room, kitchen, dining room, rec room or game room, yard, or anywhere else you gather as a family or community. In these spaces, aspects like effective communication, relationships, forgiveness, compassion, kindness, and love are important, so you need to choose crystals that support these qualities. Make a list of the ways you use your community spaces and the activities you'd like to cultivate there to determine which crystals would serve you best in these spaces.

SLEEPING AND RELAXATION SPACES

These might include places like bedrooms, bathrooms, or even a comfy couch where you like to sit and unwind. These spaces need calming and relaxing crystals that promote peace. Determine which spaces you use for this and choose crystals based on the properties listed in earlier chapters that support these spaces.

FOOD-PREPARATION AND DINING SPACES

In these spaces, such as a kitchen, an outdoor kitchen, or a family dining room, you can select crystals that support health, nutrition, well-being, good decision making, and self-love. List spaces where you prepare, serve, and eat food, including outdoor cooking and dining spaces. Then, choose crystals, based on discussions in earlier chapters, that support these spaces.

MEDITATION AND EXERCISE SPACES

In these spaces, place the appropriate crystals where you do the activity. So in exercise spaces, place energizing crystals or those that improve stamina. Crystals that allow you to relax, tune in to the Divine, or connect with a higher power are powerful in your meditation spaces. List the spaces where you perform these activities, and then consult previous chapters to determine appropriate placement and crystals.

MULTIPURPOSE SPACES

Of course, most home spaces have multiple purposes with only a few spaces dedicated to a specific activity. I recommend grouping activities of similar energies in a single space; for example, your kitchen may be a place for family to gather, where your children do homework, and where you prepare food and entertain. This, then, is a high-energy space that needs effective communication and lots of love, so choosing crystals that support these energies is essential. A bedroom might be turned into both a meditation space and a place to sleep, both which have a calm and peaceful energy.

Alternatively, in multiuse rooms, you can create zones where each activity occurs and then place crystals of the appropriate energy in those zones. Work with your family to come up with creative uses of spaces that support effective energy flow and well-being for your entire family, and then select crystals based on the agreed-upon energy you wish to draw into that space.

Intuitive Placement

I also rely on intuition for placement of crystals in my spaces. To me, if it feels like I need a specific crystal in a certain location, I place that crystal there. After I started my formal study of fêng shui, I was surprised to discover that even before I knew anything about it, I had instinctively followed many of the traditional fêng shui recommendations. My intuition had told me where the crystals needed to be before my formal education ever occurred. The moral? Never underestimate the power of your intuition. If something feels right to you, listen to that instinct.

Crystal Placement Rx for Each of the Six Areas

Let's look at how crystal placement would work for each of the six life areas where people often seek improvement.

HEALTH AND WELLNESS

For improved health and wellness, choose a crystal associated with the illness you have based on your body energetics (see chapter 5) and chakra system. Place that crystal in the center of your home, as well as in the center of any room or space where you spend a great deal of time, such as an office, living room, or bedroom.

Here's an example of bringing this all together. I have Hashimoto's thyroiditis, which has over the years progressed to become an underactive thyroid gland.

- The thyroid is associated with the throat chakra, and blue crystals support this chakra.

- I need a hexagonal crystal, which supports vitality, because I wish to improve the vitality of my thyroid.

- I need a clear crystal to amplify my thyroid energy.

- I want to place the crystal in the center of a space where I spend a great deal of time since the health area is in the very center of a space.

With this in mind, I have placed an aquamarine, which is a clear blue hexagonal crystal, under my bed, which is in the east (health area) of my bedroom, a place where I spend several hours a night. This allows me to strengthen and revitalize my thyroid gland as I sleep.

PROSPERITY AND ABUNDANCE

If you wish to improve prosperity and abundance, it's important to set up spaces with crystals that support this. Along with the fêng shui wealth area of your home, you may have areas in your home where you deal with money, such as an office space or a place where you sit and pay bills (maybe it's the kitchen table!). Therefore, you need to choose crystals associated with prosperity and place them in these locations.

As an example, let's look at my friend's office, where he works to earn a living.

- Because of the odd layout of his office space, we chose to follow the black hat fêng shui, which means his prosperity corner is in the back-left space of his office. We have placed a citrine point there, which is the best known crystal for prosperity.

- I also had him place a piece of green aventurine in his cash box to promote cash coming in.

- Finally, at his desk, where he does most of his business, he has placed a citrine cluster because the cluster will send the energy of prosperity in all directions as he works.

SELF-LOVE AND SELF-ESTEEM

For people dealing with self-esteem issues, often the kitchen, workout and meditation spaces, and bathrooms (where there are mirrors) are the hot spots where you need a boost in energy. You may also need boosts in areas where you spend time with others, where you communicate, or even where you work or create. While there isn't a "self-esteem" area of your home in fêng shui, the very center of your home is about health and well-being, so this is a good location to place stones that support self-esteem.

- Self-esteem is a third-chakra issue, which means yellow and gold stones are a good choice.

- Because you want to expand or grow your self-esteem, a monoclinic crystal is a good choice, as it supports expansion. Triclinic crystals are balancers, so you may also wish to use a triclinic crystal to balance your sense of self.

- If you have low self-esteem, you need to amplify it, which means a translucent crystal is a good choice.

Golden selenite is a yellow, transparent, monoclinic crystal, so it is a great choice to place in the center of your home or workspace to help support and nurture self-esteem. Likewise, golden labradorite is triclinic and semitransparent. Place it in the center of your desk to support a greater sense of self-worth at work.

PURPOSE (CAREER AND LIFE)

Many of us equate purpose with the work we do, so the office is a great place for using crystals that help you cultivate a sense of purpose. In your home, you could also use the bagua area of career to place a crystal.

- Purpose and developing and finding a sense of purpose is a third-chakra issue, so you'll want a crystal that is gold or yellow.

- A lack of purpose is often associated with a sense of being stuck. Orthorhombic crystals can help you unstick.

- Lack of purpose means you have an underabundance of energy, so a transparent crystal is a good choice.

Chrysoberyl is a yellow, transparent, orthorhombic crystal that can help you develop purpose and unstick you. Place some where you work and create or in the career area of your home. If your lack of purpose is related to spiritual issues, place it in the spirituality area of your home or workspace instead.

FORGIVENESS

Forgiveness is a relationship issue, so you want to focus on either the love and relationships or the family and community areas of your home or space, depending on whom you need to forgive.

- Forgiveness is a heart chakra issue, so green or pink stones are appropriate here.

- Inability to forgive is a pattern of "stuckness," which means you need to unstick. An orthorhombic crystal can help you do this.

- Inability to forgive arises from an overabundance of anger, which means you have an excess of energy. You need an opaque crystal to absorb this.

- You need a green or pink, opaque, orthorhombic crystal.

Ruby in zoisite is an opaque pink and green orthorhombic crystal. Place it in the appropriate relationship area of your home or space based on the bagua, or, if it's a spouse you need to forgive, you can place it in your bedroom. If it's an officemate or coworker, take it to work and place it at a point somewhere between the two of you.

LOVE AND RELATIONSHIPS

If you're seeking love, then using fêng shui, you'll want to place a crystal associated with love in the relationships area indicated by the bagua. If you want to strengthen your existing partnership or marriage, you can place it in your bedroom.

- Love is a heart chakra issue. You'll need a pink or green stone.

- Because you want to attract love, you'll need a tetragonal crystal, which is an attractor.

- If you are seeking love, it means you want to amplify this energy, so a transparent crystal is best.

Green apophyllite is a transparent, green tetragonal crystal, so it's excellent for attracting love relationships into your life. To strengthen or reignite an existing relationship, place the green apophyllite in your shared bedroom. To attract it, place it in the love and relationships fêng shui area of your home or space.

Space Energetics

Crystals can vastly improve the energy of spaces when you take the time to carefully consider exactly what you want to attract, select the appropriate crystal, and place it strategically in the spaces where you live and work. As I've placed crystals strategically and intuitively around my spaces, I have felt an expansion of energy, and I truly feel my life flows better and I am better able to meet my goals and obtain my desires by using crystals to facilitate an optimal flow of energy in the places where I spend most of my time. Placing crystals in my space was probably the first way I actively began to use crystals to bring about change, and it enhanced my life greatly. You can do the same by incorporating crystals into your space. Then, when you're ready to take a deeper dive, hone a new set of practices that enhance things even more…incorporating crystals into your meditation.

CHAPTER 12

Meditating with Crystals

I meditate with crystals every day. This wasn't always the case. At first, I meditated infrequently because I believed I couldn't do it well, and it felt more like a chore than a pleasure. As I studied meditation, however, I began to reframe how I thought about the practice, and I started to meditate more frequently. It wasn't until I began to incorporate crystals into my meditation, however, that everything clicked.

Many people are like I was—intimidated or bored by the idea of meditation, and I get it. I had both of those reactions. However, taking meditation from a chore to a pleasure involves a process of finding what truly works for you. And one of the best ways I've found to make this leap is by bringing crystals into my meditative activities.

Crystals and Meditation

Crystals can fulfill many purposes in meditation. For example, they can serve as a focus point, giving you something to examine with your senses as you drop into a meditative state. They can also deepen the energies you wish to cultivate in your meditation by allowing you to lock into phase, or entrain, with the crystal's specific energy. Through intention and entrainment, they serve as an excellent means of strengthening meditations focused on affirmations, visualization, or prayers. Likewise, crystals can help create a bridge to your own insight or to higher realms by raising your vibration to a level that syncs with those realms to facilitate enhanced communication. They can also assist in chakra meditation by drawing your focus to each chakra and directing energy to or from the chakras or along the chakras in a certain direction—that is, either from root to crown or crown to root. You can also use them in meditation to strengthen flow between two different chakras, such as if you need to connect your sacral chakra, where creativity is born, to your throat chakra, where creative expression occurs. I use crystals in all of these ways in my daily meditative activities, and I've found it has truly helped me embrace meditation. You can also use crystals in meditation to amplify energies you wish to cultivate, such as meditating with blue lace agate to enhance peacefulness or meditating with amethyst to amplify intuition.

In fact, crystals can direct your meditative activities in any way you wish. By using the knowledge you've gained of crystal uses and properties, you can creatively bring the appropriate crystal into meditative activities to support qualities you wish to amplify or process emotions or issues you feel you need to deal with.

The Right Way to Meditate

One of the questions my students frequently ask is about the right way to meditate. I understand the question, as it's one I asked quite a bit in my early attempts. I was always worried I wasn't doing it right. I would sit in the lotus position and try desperately to clear my typically very busy mind. For me, it was an exercise in frustration. Even when I thought I was actually succeeding at clearing my mind, I realized I was thinking about clearing my mind or what a great job I was doing at having a clear mind. Then, I discovered sitting quietly with a clear mind is only one form of meditation. There are many others, and I assure you it is possible to find the form of meditation that works for you. And so, when students ask me about the right way to meditate now, I tell them this: There is no right way to meditate. There's only the right way for you right now.

Meditative Activities

Because there seems to be such an intense focus on certain types of meditation, I've changed my language from calling it meditation to discussing "meditative activities." You'll find many activities can bring you to a meditative state, and what works for you may not work for someone else. However, in general, all of them have some common elements, including quiet contemplation and inward focus, to achieve a state of peace or enlightenment.

My definition of meditative activities, and when I use the terms "meditation" or "meditative activities" in this book, refers to the following: any practice that allows you to focus inward and be present in the moment in order to find peace, quiet the mind, grow spiritually, and allow divine guidance. I personally use many meditative practices depending on what I'm feeling in the moment; in fact, the one I use the least is sitting quietly and trying to clear my mind.

Why Meditation Is Important

The practice of meditation has many benefits. Some have been studied scientifically and show improved health, anxiety reduction, stress reduction, and improved quality of life, among many others. I also personally find daily meditation helps improve focus, it's a great time to tune in to inner wisdom and divine guidance, and it can be used as a tool for personal growth and energy healing. In my experience, working with crystals during meditative activities amps up all of these effects and helps me achieve meditative states more easily.

How Often to Do It

I believe in making meditation a daily practice, one you undertake as often as you can for as long as you can. If this means you can do five minutes a day, perfect. If it means you can chunk it into three or four five-minute increments, great! If you find you have more time or more desire, do more. If it occasionally (or frequently) turns into what I like to call "napitation" (falling asleep while meditating), no worries. I try to aim for about 20 minutes or more most days. Some of my meditations last longer, and some are shorter. Sometimes I do it in shorter chunks; occasionally, I have a marathon session of an hour or more, and it turns into a nap not infrequently. Occasionally, I don't get around to it and wind up skipping a day.

I've found that working with crystals helps increase the frequency and duration of my meditations. Crystals often give me something to focus on, move me into an altered state more quickly, or just make the entire process feel better. It's why I believe they are such an excellent tool for engaging in meditative activities: because they increase overall engagement and amplify the effects in such a way that instead of meditation being a chore, it becomes something I look forward to doing. Since I've started meditating with crystals, I can't imagine not meditating, which is a far cry from where I started.

Types of Meditative Activities

There are many types of meditative activities. In fact, I'm sure there are many I have yet to identify, since how one attains a meditative state is highly individualized. There are far more types than those I outline here. If you find a practice that quiets your mind and works for you, then I recommend incorporating it into your practice, whether it's something I've listed here or not.

TRADITIONAL MEDITATION

Traditional meditation is the form most people think of when they hear the term "meditation." Holding or gazing at a crystal can enhance this form of meditation because you can focus on the sensation of the crystal in your hand or hold the image of the crystal in your mind when you feel it drift. A good third eye chakra crystal, like amethyst, is excellent for focus meditation, and amethyst also has the benefit of being calming and providing clarity. If you can find it, Brandenberg amethyst, which is a combination of amethyst, clear quartz, and smoky quartz, is a particularly powerful stone for mindfulness meditation. Clear quartz can also help amplify focus.

To use crystals in traditional meditation:

1. Sit or lie quietly and comfortably holding a crystal in your receiving hand, which is your nondominant hand.

2. Focusing on the feeling of the crystal in your hand, clear your mind of any thoughts.

3. As you sit quietly, notice any thoughts as they arise.

4. Don't judge yourself when you notice thoughts. Simply release them.

5. If you find your focus wandering, return your attention to the crystal in your hand or visualize its image in your mind.

In this type of meditation, additional imagery may help you release thoughts that come up. For example, visualize the thoughts as written words on a chalkboard and visualize erasing them before focusing on your crystal once again. Alternatively, when you notice a thought, you could think, *Release*, and allow it to drift away.

MANTRA MEDITATION

In mantra meditation with a crystal, you use a word or phrase as your point of focus and hold a crystal that enhances that focus in your receiving, or nondominant, hand.

1. Chant your mantra silently or aloud throughout the duration of the meditation.

2. If you notice thoughts intruding, gently return your attention to your mantra and the feel of the crystal in your hand.

Your mantra can be a single word or phrase, such as the traditional "om, om shanti shanti shanti," or "om mani padme hum," which are traditional Eastern meditation mantras, or it can be an affirmation or quality you'd like to develop, such as "peace," or "I am healthy, happy, and prosperous." Choose a mantra that is meaningful to you (see chapter 18 for more ideas).

Some crystal and mantra pairings include:

•   "Om shanti shanti shanti" is an invocation of peace. Choose rainbow fluorite or blue lace agate or crystals that promote peace.

•   "Om mani padme hum" is a Tibetan Buddhist mantra that evokes enlightenment. With this mantra, choose a crown chakra crystal with a high vibration, such as phenacite or apophyllite.

Bija seed mantras are single-syllable mantras that activate and balance each chakra. Typically, you focus on a single bija mantra during a meditation, and you can pair a crystal with each mantra.

•   "Lam" (lahm) balances the root chakra. Choose red hematite.

•   "Vam" (vahm) balances the sacral chakra. Meditate with carnelian.

•   "Ram" (rrham with a rolled r) balances the solar plexus chakra. Hold a piece of citrine.

- "Yam" (yahm) balances the heart chakra. Hold a piece of green tourmaline.

- "Ham" (hahm) balances the throat chakra. Meditate with a piece of lapis lazuli.

- "Om" (aum or ohm) balances the third eye chakra. Meditate with amethyst.

- Silence balances the crown chakra. Focus on clear quartz.

FOCUS MEDITATION

Like mantra meditation, focus meditation gives you something to focus on to keep your mind clear. You can focus on anything from one of the five senses, such as a scent or music, but you can also use a crystal. A clear crystal cut into a sphere with lots of inclusions, such as a piece of smoky quartz or citrine, makes an excellent focus point.

1. Place the crystal in front of you where you can see it clearly with a soft gaze. Minimize other distractions.

2. With a soft gaze, focus on the crystal. Breathe deeply.

3. As you feel your focus wander, return your sight to the crystal once more. Every time your attention wanders, without judgment, bring it gently back to the crystal in front of you.

MOVEMENT MEDITATION

Meditation with crystals doesn't have to occur seated in the lotus position. In fact, you don't even need to be seated to do it. One of my favorite meditation practices is movement meditation. I use a form of dance called Nia for my movement meditation, and I remain focused on my movements and the music. I always have a smooth grounding crystal of some sort in my sports bra, around my neck, or in a pocket if I have one, since the intention of a movement meditation is connection to the earth and grounding. When my mind wanders, I bring it back to that activity. Other forms of movement meditation include any repetitive movements, such as walking or running, yoga, and similar forms of activity.

For movement meditation, choose a grounding crystal such as dark smoky quartz or a garnet. If you don't have a place on your person to wear it, put it in a pouch around your neck. Focus on your movements, noticing how the crystal helps connect you to the energy of the earth.

AFFIRMATION

Affirmations fall soundly into a category of meditation you'll sometimes see called Western meditation. Affirmation is a very powerful, active form of meditation that allows you to focus on energetic shifts you wish to make in your life. In my crystal meditations, I always start and finish with

affirmations.

For the most powerful way to perform affirmation meditation, choose one or two affirmations you wish to focus on throughout the duration of your meditation, as well as crystals that support the energy of those affirmations using the information you've learned about selecting crystals in previous chapters.

Make your affirmation a positive statement as opposed to a negative one. For example, if you are working on your health, you might affirm, "I am healthy, happy, and strong," as opposed to, "I am not sick." Then, choose a crystal that supports the energy of the affirmation.

To perform the affirmation, sit or lie comfortably, hold the crystal in your receiving hand, and breathe deeply. Notice the energy of the crystal in your hand as you repeat your affirmation silently or aloud. If you feel your mind wander, return to the affirmation and focus on the crystal.

We will cover affirmations in more depth in chapter 18.

VISUALIZATION

Visualization with crystals is a powerful way to manifest change in your life. Frequently, my visualizations involve moving energy through my chakras in order to balance them, but you can also visualize things you wish to manifest in your life. To visualize with a crystal:

1. Choose a crystal that supports the energy you wish to bring about with your visualization based on what you've learned about selecting crystals in previous chapters. Hold it in your receiving hand.

2. Sit or lie comfortably. Visualize energy coming from the crystal and entering into your hand and into your body, bringing the energy you desire.

3. Visualize that energy flowing into every cell of your body. Now, move your focus from the crystal's energy to what it is you would like to see in your life. Imagine yourself and how you would be and feel if you had already achieved it. Spend time visualizing this in detail.

4. When you're ready, return your focus to the crystal energy flowing through you once again.

PRAYER

Prayer with crystals doesn't have to be in its traditional form during meditation. You can talk to God, Buddha, Jesus, or whatever figure is important to you. Alternatively, you can contemplate principles that are important to you, such as using Zen koans. For this type of meditation, use a crystal that connects you to a higher power, such as Super Seven or phenacite.

I use a form of prayer in my daily meditation. As a Reiki master, I meditate daily on the five Reiki principles—I will not worry, I will not anger, I will be grateful, I will be kind to all living things, I will do my work honestly—and I start meditation with this before moving into affirmation, visualization, or other forms of meditation. It is my form of prayer, and I hold a special crystal called a Vogel crystal that is cut in a specific geometric shape to enhance communication with higher realms.

LIVING MEDITATION

Another of my favorite forms of meditation with crystals is something I call living meditation, and it's simply being focused in the present moment regardless of what you are doing, maintaining your focus on your task and allowing other thoughts to drift away. Clear quartz is an excellent crystal for this—wear it or carry it in a pocket. Before you do, hold it in your hands for a few moments, close your eyes, and intend for the crystal to keep you focused and mindful of the present moment. Then, wear it or stick it in a pocket and go about your day.

This is a great form of meditation for people who believe they don't have time to meditate. It works well when you are performing mundane tasks, such as showering, preparing a meal, brushing your teeth, washing dishes, or folding laundry. As you perform the task, focus first on the intention you set for the crystal in your pocket. Once you have connected, start to focus on the sensory input. For example, if you are folding laundry, notice the feel of the laundry as you touch it. Notice its scent and the sounds of folding. Focus on making precise folds and stacking it neatly. If your attention wanders, return it to the sensory input of your task.

GUIDED MEDITATION

Guided meditation is another form that works well for people who don't believe they can meditate. You can incorporate a crystal by choosing one that will help you with your listening skills, such as any throat chakra stone. Good examples include sodalite, lapis lazuli, and celestite. Lie down during this meditation and place the crystal directly on or next to your throat chakra.

You can find many guided meditations online and via smartphone apps. See "Resources" for my favorite apps, or do some research and find those that work for you.

During guided meditation, you use the voice of the person guiding you as your point of focus, visualizing what they are saying to keep your mind focused and intent. You can also use hypnosis recordings as a form of guided meditation to help you accomplish specific things, such as smoking cessation or pain management. If the guided meditation affects a certain chakra or has a specific intent, choose a stone based on what you have learned in previous chapters to support that specific chakra or intent.

Incorporating Crystals into Your Meditation

When you add a crystal to your meditation, it can help improve focus and provide desired energy to support your meditation goals, such as communicating with your higher self, achieving peace, or being healthier.

When working with a crystal in meditation, you'll want to choose one that supports the energy of your overall goal. The following meditations offer specific instructions for meditation practices to support each of the six life areas as well as crystals that you can use to deepen the meditations and strengthen the energy of intention.

Crystal Meditation for
Health and Wellness

Choose green crystals, those associated with the chakra linked to the health issue you wish to fix based on what you've learned in previous chapters, or a crystal, such as turquoise, that supports overall health, healing, and vitality. Use a freshly cleansed crystal.

1. Lie comfortably on your back with the crystal placed on the location that needs healing or on the appropriate chakra. If it is for overall health, then place the crystal next to you or, if you are on a bed or table, under the pillow or under the center of your body.

2. Start by breathing deeply, in through the nose and out through your mouth, focusing on your breath.

3. When you feel peace, visualize green healing light entering through the crown of your head and flowing downward into your body. Watch it move through every body part and see it filling every cell. Do this for as long as you need or until you feel guided to stop.

4. Now return your focus to your breathing. Visualize breathing in the healing light on each inhale and releasing any illness on the exhale. Again, do this for as long as you need.

5. When you are ready, visualize white light entering on your breath and filling you. Give thanks for your healing and open your eyes when you are ready.

6. Cleanse your crystal.

Crystal Meditation for Prosperity and Abundance

Visualization is an excellent tool for prosperity because it helps you create a prosperity mindset. Choose a newly cleansed appropriate prosperity crystal, such as citrine, or a green crystal like green aventurine.

1. Sit comfortably and hold the crystal in your receiving hand (your nondominant hand, typically the left hand; although for lefties, it's the right hand).

2. Breathe in through your nose and out through your mouth, focusing for a moment on your breathing until you feel safe, comfortable, and relaxed.

3. Now, focus on your crystal. Feel its energy entering through your hands, flowing throughout your being, and surrounding you.

4. As you feel the crystal's energy flowing into you and surrounding you, begin to visualize the field it creates as a giant magnet that attracts prosperity.

5. See money flowing to your giant magnet from all angles, and flowing from your magnet to you. Do this for as long as you wish.

6. When you are ready, return your focus to your crystal and your breathing.

7. Affirm, "I give thanks to the universe that I am prosperous."

8. When you are ready, open your eyes.

9. Cleanse your crystal.

Crystal Meditation for
Self-Love and Self-Esteem

Mantra meditations can be powerful for boosting self-esteem. I recommend freshly cleansed yellow tigers eye or yellow amber for this meditation, although you can choose any crystal to which you are drawn that supports self-esteem (typically a gold or yellow crystal). You'll need to have a mirror where you can see it comfortably, as your eyes will be your focus point here along with your mantra.

1. Sit or stand comfortably near a mirror where you can see your eyes. Hold the crystal in your hands, pressing it to your solar plexus chakra.

2. Meet your own eyes in the mirror.

3. Breathe in through your nose and out through your mouth for a few moments until you feel calm and relaxed. Maintain focus on your eyes.

4. Repeat the mantra in your mind or aloud on each breath, "I love myself unconditionally."

5. Do this for as long as feels comfortable.

6. Cleanse your crystal.

Crystal Meditation for
Purpose (Career and Life)

This meditation can help you connect with your divine self for guidance to help you find a sense of purpose. Use a freshly cleansed amethyst or another third eye crystal, such as charoite, sugilite, or lepidolite.

1. Lie comfortably on your back with your eyes closed. Place your crystal on your third eye.

2. Breathe deeply in through your nose and out through your mouth.

3. When you feel safe, relaxed, and comfortable, say aloud or in your mind, "Tell me what I need to know."

4. Then, focus on your third eye just below your crystal, visualizing a screen there in your mind and noticing any pictures, colors, or other information that appears on the screen.

5. As thoughts arise, gently release them and return your focus to the screen.

6. Do this for as long as is comfortable.

7. When you are done, say, "Thank you," and open your eyes.

8. Cleanse your crystal.

Crystal Meditation for Forgiveness

Choose a freshly cleansed heart stone, like emerald or malachite, for this visualization meditation. Since forgiveness is all about removing blocked love energy and returning to a place of love and compassion, heart chakra stones are essential in strengthening loving energy.

1. Sit comfortably holding the stone to your heart chakra with both hands. Breathe in through your nose and out through your mouth.

2. Feel the energy of the stone enter through your heart chakra and fill your body.

3. Now, visualize the person you need to forgive. Notice energetic ties running from you to them tying you together.

4. Imagine taking a pair of scissors and cutting each of those ties one at a time. As you cut each tie, say aloud or in your mind, "I release you."

5. After you have cut all the ties, visualize that person surrounded with golden light. Surround yourself with the same light.

6. When you are ready, open your eyes.

7. Cleanse your crystal.

Crystal Meditation for
Love and Relationships

Love and relationships are centered in your heart chakra, so pink stones, such as morganite or rose quartz, work well for this meditation. Be sure to select a freshly cleansed stone. You will need two of the same stone for this meditation.

1. Hold one stone in each hand—one for giving and one for receiving.

2. Sit or lie comfortably with your eyes closed, breathing in through your nose and out through your mouth.

3. Focus first on the stone in your dominant (giving) hand. Feel love flow from your heart, down through your arm, into your hand, and into the stone. Notice the stone grow warm with the energy you are sending it, and visualize it expanding out from the stone and surrounding you with pink light. See the love go all the way out from you, expanding into your aura, and then into the room and out into the universe.

4. Visualize the pink light traveling from your giving hand around the planet, gathering and sharing love, and returning to the stone in your receiving hand. Feel the stone grow warm with the energy of love.

5. Now, visualize that love flowing in through your hand, up your arm, and into your heart. Continue cycling the love through the stones, out into the universe, and back into you for as long as feels appropriate.

6. When you are ready, open your eyes.

7. Cleanse your stone.

Grounding After Meditation

It's important to ground yourself after any meditation to return you to your body and bring you back to earth so you can go about your day with focus. To do this, sit or stand with your feet flat on the floor and hold a grounding crystal, such as black tourmaline or hematite, in your receiving, or non-dominant, hand. Visualize roots growing from the bottom of your feet and into the earth. You only need to do this for a moment or two.

Listen to Your Intuition

While I've performed every one of the meditations above at some point, I often follow my intuition for meditation. I keep an array of crystals within reach in my meditation space, so if I intuitively realize I need one, I can reach for it without too much interruption. Sometimes during my meditation, a specific crystal will arise into my mind, and I know I need to use it. Fortunately, I know most of my meditation crystals by feel (I keep seven nearby, one for each chakra), so if morganite arises in my mind, I can maintain my position, reach for it without opening my eyes, and continue onward.

Before every meditation, I take a moment, close my eyes, tune in, and ask, "What do I need right now?" I highly recommend doing this. Ask, focus on your breathing, and if a specific crystal arises in your mind, use it in your meditation.

Developing Your Own Rituals

I view meditative activities as a ritual, and crystals are part of that ritual. Over time, my rituals have changed and adapted as my needs have. The meditative activities I've shared with you have served me well, but as time passes, they evolve and change according to what I intuitively understand I need. So if none of these meditations resonates with you, it's okay. They serve as a good starting point, but they aren't the only meditative activities available. Listen to your intuition and use your own rituals and meditations to increase energies you desire in your life. The more you tune in, the more your intuition as to the meditative activities and rituals you need will grow. The important thing is to create a practice that works for you and helps you feel focused, centered, and empowered to choose crystals, rituals, and practices that meet your needs, whether placing crystals in your environment, using them for meditation, or wearing them with purpose.

CHAPTER 13

Wearing Crystals

Because I am a fan of all things sparkly, I love wearing crystals. Wearing them makes me happy. It's also a good way to ensure I have crystal energy with me throughout my day no matter where I go. Therefore, I wholeheartedly recommend wearing crystals. However, I also suggest you do so with intention and purpose instead of just grabbing any old crystal that pleases the eye. My husband Jim recently discovered this was true.

Jim is not a guy who, when I met him, would ever have dreamed of wearing crystals. I call him Techie McScienceGeek because he has a background in nuclear engineering, and he is an incredibly rational human being. For years, he has politely listened to my jibber jabber about crystals and then gone on about his very rational day.

Recently, something happened in his life that made him extremely angry. The anger started to consume him, and he had trouble letting go of it. One day he trailed me into one of my regular crystal shops, where I started chatting with the store's owner about a type of precisely cut crystal jewelry called Tools for Evolution. As we chatted, she turned to Jim and gestured to his heart and solar plexus region, saying, "When you're ready to deal with this whole thing, let me know."

After we left, I tactfully fielded his questions about what she could have possibly meant by "this whole thing," suggesting it might have something to do with his current anger issues. A few days later, Jim decided he might be ready to "deal with this whole thing." So we went on the store's website and looked at the Tools for Evolution they had available. Before even looking, I suggested he might need a particular cut called the Flower of Life, which helps bring joy, in a citrine stone, which is a stone that can help release anger. However, his eye was drawn to a different cut and stone, and he was certain that was the one he needed.

The next day, we headed back to the store. He told the owner he was ready to deal, and he knew exactly what he wanted, naming the cut and stone. She had other ideas and told him, "Let's try this. I'm going to put these in your hands with your eyes closed so you can't see what they are, and you see which feels best for you." She did this with several cuts and stones, including the one he had chosen and the one she felt was best for him, which, not surprisingly, was also the one I had chosen. He picked the one the store owner and I had originally chosen and started wearing it under his shirt where nobody could see it.

According to Jim, his anger just melted away. He wears that tool every day now along with another one he later picked out in the same manner, sometimes even outside of his shirt where others can see it. He says the pendant helps him feel balanced and peaceful, and he finds it is easier to let go of anger now, although it is something he has struggled with all of his life. He is also more in touch with his other emotions, which is also new for him. The crystals have been very effective at giving Jim what he most needed when he most needed it.

Jim's story illustrates an important point. For years, Jim was highly skeptical about wearing or using crystals. However, an untenable situation finally allowed him to soften his stance, but even then, he tried to reason his way to finding an appropriate crystal.

He picked out what he thought would be best for him based on which one he thought looked the best. However, when Jim allowed himself to feel the energy of the crystal without looking at it, he found he was far more in touch with his intuition than he could have imagined. The crystal he picked by "feel" instead of sight made a huge difference in his state of mind, and it gave him exactly the tools he needed to move beyond what had been a very stubborn blockage.

Jim thought he rationally knew what he needed, which at first wasn't a crystal and then was a specific-looking crystal. It was only when he set those preconceived ideas aside and allowed himself to feel that he was able to move past the blockage. Since Jim refers to himself as a "psychic lead-lined bank vault," so if he can intuit what he needs and allow himself to wear crystals in order to shift energetically, you can too. Listen to your intuition and allow the crystal's energy to speak to you in order to facilitate change.

Where to Wear Crystals on Your Body

The first rule of thumb is this: wear crystals on your body wherever it instinctively feels best. There are also some general guidelines that can aid your specific intentions.

EARRINGS

When you wear crystals in your ears, they support your upper chakras best, from your throat to your crown. Therefore, blue, violet, and clear crystals work well here, as do high vibration crystals. Amethyst, clear quartz, diamonds, iolite, sapphire, morganite, aquamarine, and tanzanite are all good earring choices.

Of the six major life areas we've identified, wearing crystal earrings are most helpful with purpose or with health issues from the throat upward, such as:

- For the mouth, choose blue crystals.

- For the jaw, choose blue crystals.

- For issues associated with the ears, choose blue crystals.

- For eye issues, select violet or purple crystals.

- For sinuses, select violet or purple.

- For issues associated with the throat, wear blue crystals.

- For headaches, choose violet, purple, clear, or white.

- Amethyst is excellent for sleep issues.

- Violet, purple, and white crystals can help with mental disorders.

- For issues of cognition, choose violet, purple, clear, or white.

- If you have musculoskeletal issues, choose white or clear crystals.

- White or clear crystals can also help with systemic problems.

For example, my favorite earrings are tanzanite crystals. I call them my "phone home" earrings because when I wear them, they heighten my intuitive abilities and help me focus on higher guidance.

NECKLACES AND PENDANTS

One of the great things about necklaces and pendants is you can direct where the energy goes by the length of the chain. If you have a chain that is long enough (about 28 to 32 inches), it can rest over your heart chakra, which is the center of your chakra system. This is a great length for multi-colored stones that balance energies along the chakra system, such as rainbow fluorite, watermelon tourmaline, or snowflake obsidian.

Pendants on shorter chains are beneficial for issues associated with the throat and heart chakras, while very long chains can help issues associated with the solar plexus chakra.

Of the six primary intention areas we've identified, pendants work best for health, self-esteem, forgiveness, and love.

Health. This, as always, depends on the health issue. Pendants are best for issues associated with:

- throat chakra (blue stones, such as iolite)

- heart chakra (green or pink stones, such as malachite and kunzite)

- solar plexus chakra (golden or yellow stones, such as citrine, pyrite, and tigers eye)

Adjust the chain length so the stone is closest to the chakra that governs the health area you are trying to help.

Forgiveness. Choose a green or pink opaque pendant on a longer chain that falls in the vicinity of the heart chakra. Ruby in fuchsite or ruby in zoisite are good stones for this, as is malachite, aventurine, jade, or amazonite.

Love. Choose a translucent green or pink stone (or a combination) on a longer chain, such as watermelon tourmaline, rainbow fluorite, emerald, or morganite.

BRACELETS AND ANKLETS

Crystals on bracelets can help with issues of the solar plexus, sacral, and root chakras, as well as issues associated with the arms, hands, and fingers, as well the hips, legs, ankles, feet, and toes. Anklets are best for the legs, hips, and feet, as well as the root chakra. Choose red, orange, brown, gold, and black crystals for bracelets, and black, brown, or red crystals for anklets.

Of the six issues we've identified, bracelet crystals work best for self-esteem and prosperity, as well as for health problems arising from the solar plexus downward.

Health. Choose crystals in bracelets that support the individual health problem and its associated chakras, such as:

- For blood disorders, choose bloodstone or hematite.

- For foot or ankle pain, select black or red stones, like garnet and black tourmaline.

174

- For gastrointestinal issues, choose orange or brown stones, such as carnelian or smoky quartz.

- For issues of your abdominal organs, select orange, brown, or red stones, such as red jasper, Boji Stones, or peach moonstone.

- For mental health issues, like depression or anxiety, wear black and white stones, like Dalmatian jasper or snowflake obsidian.

Prosperity. Choose prosperity stones, like citrine or green stones, or choose orange stones, like dark amber, to remove sacral chakra blocks to prosperity.

Self-esteem. Choose yellow or gold stones, such as yellow tigers eye or topaz for bracelets.

RINGS

Rings follow the same suggestions as bracelets above, but you can also be more directed with rings because according to the ancient art of palmistry, each hand and each finger has a symbolic meaning. Therefore, wearing a crystal ring on a specific hand and finger can direct energy more intentionally than any other location where you might wear a crystal on your body.

- Your left hand is your receiving hand (unless you are left-hand dominant; then, reverse this).

- Your right hand is your giving hand (unless you are left-hand dominant; then, reverse this).

- Your left hand is also associated with your subconscious mind.

- Your right hand is associated with your active, analytical mind.

- Your thumbs are associated with willpower and self-nurturing.

- Your pointer fingers are associated with desire and ambition.

- Your middle fingers are associated with power and self-identity.

- Your ring fingers are associated with commitment, love, and creativity.

- Your pinkies are associated with boundaries and relationships.

So, where you wear your rings can have different symbolic meanings. Let's look at this with our six areas in mind.

Health. If you are a healer, wear rings associated with healing, such as healer quartz, on the thumb (nurture finger) or middle finger (self, power) of your giving hand. You may also want to wear a protective stone, like hematite, on the pinkie (boundaries) of your receiving hand so you don't absorb illness from those you work with. Alternatively, if you need healing, wear a stone associated with healing, such as turquoise, clear quartz, or healer quartz, on the pointer finger (finger of desire, want, and ambition) of your receiving hand in order to set your intention for health and receive it. You can also wear a ring associated with the chakra of the issue you are trying to heal on that finger.

Prosperity. Wear a prosperity stone, such as green aventurine, on the desire finger of your receiving hand. For example, I wear a citrine ring on my right (receiving) hand pointer (ambition and desire) finger. It is pear-shaped with the wide part away from my body and the pointed part pointing at my hand, which draws prosperity energy from the universe into the wide part of the pear and funnels it down my desire finger, into my receiving hand through the point, and into the rest of my body.

Self-esteem. Wear golden or yellow stones associated with self-esteem, such as tigers eye, on the middle (self) and boundary (pinkie) fingers of your receiving hand.

Purpose. Wear a communication stone, such as amethyst, on the ambition (pointer) or self (middle) finger of your receiving hand.

Forgiveness. Wear an emerald or rose quartz stone on the love (ring) finger of your giving hand.

Love and relationships. Wear a morganite or ruby ring on the ambition and desire (pointer) or love and commitment (ring) finger of your receiving hand and wear a small black stone, such as black tourmaline, on the pinkie (boundaries and love) of your giving hand so you don't lose yourself in love.

Fashion Versus Focus

Of course, you can wear any crystal jewelry because you like how it looks as well. Just be clear on whether you are wearing a crystal because you like the way it looks (fashion) or because it has a specific intention. There is no right or wrong way to do this, but it's important to understand that without focus, your crystals will be less likely to bring about the change you'd like to see.

CAN YOU WEAR TOO MANY CRYSTALS?

I'm just going to go ahead and say no because I love sparkle, and I just counted. I'm wearing 18 crystals at the moment as I casually sit around in my sweatpants typing on my computer. So have at it, but with a caveat. While wearing a bunch of different crystals won't cancel each other out, sometimes if you wear certain combinations of crystals, you may send the universe confusing messages. For example, if you're seeking love and wear a morganite ring on the desire finger of your receiving hand but have the rest of your body draped in a crystal that repels energy, such as hematite, your message may be a bit confusing for the universe.

Therefore, if you're trying to create certain energy in your life, I recommend you carefully consider which crystals you wear and how you wear them in order to create the intention and space for the change you wish to enter your life.

Likewise, you may want to time when you wear certain crystals. For example, if you wear a fiery crystal or one with a lot of high energy to sleep, it may cause issues. If you find yourself having sleep problems when you are wearing crystals, try taking a few of the more energetic crystals—such as reds, oranges, and blacks—off and see if it helps. For instance, Jim cannot sleep in his Tools for Evolution pendant, so he removes it every night. I had trouble sleeping in mine the first day or two, but as I got used to the energy, I was able to wear mine to sleep. It's up to you; if they don't bother you, wear them to sleep. If they do, remove them.

CLEANSING CRYSTALS YOU WEAR

Finally, a quick note about wearing crystals. When they travel with you and are on your body all day long, they work hard for you and need more frequent cleansing than other crystals. To keep them in tip-top shape, I recommend daily cleansing (see chapter 10, "Caring for and Maintaining Your Crystals").

LISTEN TO YOUR GUIDANCE

When in doubt, do this: Hold a piece of crystal jewelry in your receiving hand and close your eyes. Focus on the crystal and ask aloud or in your mind, "Is this the right crystal for me to wear today?" Then listen to the intuitive responses from your divine guidance system and proceed as directed. Ultimately, regardless of any "rules" or tips I offer, remember this: You know best what you need. So if wearing a certain crystal feels right to you, do it until it stops feeling right. Then choose something else.

CHAPTER 14

Using Crystals in Combinations

Crystals can work together synergistically to create an energy that is better than the sum of its parts. Some combinations strengthen and support the energy of each to make their intention and vibration stronger or more specifically focused.

Bonus Crystals

In the world of cooking, we have a saying, "If it grows together, it goes together," which essentially means when two food products grow in close proximity, they often complement one another in taste. Mother Nature is that smart with food, and is also that intelligent with crystals. I'm a huge fan of what I call bonus crystals, which are crystals that have more than one type of crystal in them. I have several of these types of crystals, where one crystal has grown in a matrix of the other crystal.

Some examples of bonus crystals I have include:

- aquamarine in clear quartz
- aquamarine in smoky quartz
- calcite in amethyst
- red hematite and rutile in amethyst
- rutile in hematite
- stilbite in apophyllite
- tourmaline in amethyst
- tourmaline in morganite

These are just a few examples of crystals that grow together, and in doing so they create a unique vibration that is different from each individual crystal.

A really good example of this is a stone called Super Seven or Melody's Stone. It is a combination of seven different crystals that all grow into one stone (amethyst, clear quartz, smoky quartz, cacoxenite, rutile, goethite, and lepidocrocite). Any of these single stones has a unique vibration, but when they combine together in Super Seven, they are incredibly powerful. Super Seven is an extremely high-vibration stone that connects you to higher realms and can help you have visions or communicate with the Divine.

Septarian, sometimes called dragon eggs, is another stone that combines multiple crystals, including golden calcite, aragonite, and limestone. It has a powerful grounding energy that connects and balances the first three chakras. While each crystal has its own properties, when they are combined, they create one highly grounding and protective stone.

Crystal Synergies

There are many, many, many synergistic crystal combinations, so I'll offer six, one for each of our areas.

Health and wellness. Clear quartz is perhaps one of the best general healing stones that brings good health and energy. It also amplifies energy. Therefore, it is powerful to combine it with any stone for a specific health condition to make that energy stronger and more healing.

Prosperity and abundance. Citrine is one of the most powerful stones for attracting prosperity, but blocks to prosperity actually occur in the second chakra. Therefore, combining aragonite, a second-chakra stone that removes blockages because it's orthorhombic, with the citrine makes a powerful combination to clear any energetic blockages to abundance while attracting wealth.

Self-love and self-esteem. While self-esteem is primarily a third-chakra issue that can be supported by gold or yellow stones, lack of self-love may also be at issue. Therefore, combining a stone of unconditional love, such as rose quartz, with a self-esteem supporting stone, like tigers eye, is a powerful combination.

Purpose. Purple stones help you find purpose because they provide divine guidance, but creativity for problem solving originates in your sacral chakra. Therefore, combining a sacral chakra stone, like sunstone, with a third eye chakra stone, like iolite, can create a powerful shift in finding purpose. As a bonus, you can often find iolite stones that contain sunstone or sunstones that contain iolite, so there's no need to purchase two stones.

Forgiveness. Many people don't realize that forgiveness is an act of self-love, so in order to truly forgive, you need to have enough sense of self-worth to make the choice to let go. So while rhodonite or another pink or green crystal is an excellent gemstone for forgiveness, it helps to combine it with a crystal that supports self-love, such as citrine.

Love and relationships. To bring love into your life, there's nothing better than rose quartz. However, before you can find new love, you must let go of hurt associated with past loves, which is where malachite comes in. Malachite will help you move past any lingering hurt from past love while rose quartz will attract new love.

Crystal Grids

Another way to combine crystals to create a powerful vibrational intention is with a crystal grid. A crystal grid is a grouping of crystals laid out in a geometric pattern with a specific energetic intention. For example, when I teach my classes, I lay out a simple circular crystal grid with a center stone of fluorite to enhance my ability to communicate effectively and a circular perimeter of blue calcite stones to enhance learning for my students.

Grids work for two reasons. First, they involve the strategic combination of crystals so the properties of each crystal can enhance, direct, focus, and strengthen the properties of the others. Next, they rely on geometric shapes that convey specific intention or meaning. The combination of geometry and crystal synergy work together to create powerful and directed energy.

You can lay grids anywhere you wish to create specific energies in your home, workspace, or play spaces. For instance, when I perform Reiki sessions, I sometimes create grids with multiple stones to facilitate chakra balance or healing energies under my treatment table. These might be simple, such as a line of chakra stones under the table, or they may be a more complex geometric or representational shape, such as a heart shape for love or a spiral for spiritual growth and awakening. In this way, grids provide a way of synergistically combining multiple crystals to strengthen a specific intention.

Grids can be as simple or as complex as you wish. I've made them with just two layers, and I've made them with eight or nine different layers moving outward from the center.

It's easy to create your own grids with a few guidelines.

THE CENTER STONE IS THE FOCUS STONE

Determine the focus of your grid—the main energy you wish to draw—and based on that, select a focus stone. This becomes the center stone of your grid. For example, if your grid is focused on attracting love, use a rose quartz as your focus stone.

INNER RINGS AROUND THE FOCUS STONE CLARIFY AND REFINE INTENTION

You may just have one ring around your focus stone, or you may have multiple rings. Each clarifies or adds to your intention. For instance, with your love grid, you may want to attract someone with whom you communicate well. In that case, you'd place communication stones, such as blue calcite, around the center stone. You can do this with additional rings, as well. If you wanted to cultivate joy in the relationship, as well, then the next layer might be carnelian, which brings joy and happiness. You can create as many layers of stones around the center stone as you wish.

THE STONES AROUND THE PERIMETER DIRECT OR CONFINE ENERGY

Perimeter stones may be used to contain energy, such as using black tourmaline in an outer perimeter of a grid to keep the energy confined to the space. For example, perhaps you create a grid to help rid yourself of nightmares by placing it underneath your bed. The center stone or inner rings might contain stones that absorb negativity, such as hematite, and then by placing a ring of black tourmaline around the perimeter, you can ensure the energy remains contained within the hematite instead of moving outward into the room. These types of grids are excellent for shadow work, where you are trying to release negative energy in order to move forward in a positive direction.

Alternatively, you may wish to amplify or direct the energy created by the grid by placing clear quartz points pointed outward from the perimeter to direct energy from the grid outward and into the universe. So in your romance and love grid from above, you may want to place a perimeter of clear quartz points pointing in every direction outward to send your intention out into the universe.

GRID SHAPES DERIVE MEANING FROM SYMBOLISM OR SACRED GEOMETRY

You can create your grid in a meaningful shape to refine the purpose further. For example, you could make your romance grid in the shape of a heart. You can also find grid cloths, commercially called a grid layout or just a crystal grid, that have sacred geometry shapes on them for laying out more complex grids. Shape meanings for grids include:

- Hearts represent love.

- The infinity symbol represents the infinite, the Divine, or an unending cycle.

- Circles represent balance, oneness, and grounding.

- Spirals represent creativity, spiritual growth, and walking a path.

- A vesica piscis (two interlinked circles) represents infinity, duality, and balance.

- Bromean rings (three interlocked circles arranged in a pyramid) represent teamwork and family.

- A triquetra or Celtic knot (the center of the Bromean rings) represents creativity, balance, and protection.

- A seed of life (seven overlapping circles arranged in a circular pattern) represents truth and creation.

- Metatron's cube or a Merkabah (13 overlapping circles) represents divinity.

- Flower of life represents recognition of self as divine.

- A pentagram represents connection to the Earth.

- A Star of David represents compassion and kindness.

GRIDS FOR THE SIX AREAS

Without going too far overboard (because making grids is cool and creative, and they can become unwieldly quickly or require you to buy a ton of crystals), I offer a few simple grids for each of our six areas. I've tried to use commonly available, affordable stones because you'll need to buy more than one of them for some of the grids.

Health and wellness. Create a simple circle grid for balance in health. In the center, place a stone associated with your specific health problem. Then, create a perimeter of clear quartz points pointing outward into the universe. You can also place this grid under your bed and stand the quartz points on end, pointing up at you.

Prosperity and abundance. Create a grid for growing prosperity by making a spiral. Start with a citrine crystal as the center of the spiral, and then spiral outward with small pieces of green aventurine. At the open end of the spiral, place a double-terminated (point on each end) clear quartz point to amplify the energy and draw it both from the universe and from the grid.

Self-love and self-esteem. Create a Star of David grid. In the center, place the intention stone for self-esteem, citrine. Around it in the shape of the star (or at least for each of the star points), place red-orange carnelian, which helps strengthen your sense of self.

Purpose. An infinity symbol will represent the eternal and cyclical nature of purpose. Your focus stone should be the intersection between the two loops of the infinity sign. Choose amethyst here, which will summon divine guidance. On one loop, use carnelian to summon creativity. In the other loop, use blue calcite to help you communicate your purpose and bring it into action.

Forgiveness. The Star of David is a good shape for forgiveness because it represents compassion, which is required for forgiveness. Place rose quartz in the center of the star, and for each of the points, place a piece of smoky quartz to transmute negative energy to positive and release stuck energy.

Love and relationships. Although it may seem cheesy, a heart-shaped grid is effective here. Use rose quartz in the center of the heart and then make a heart shape with carnelian to bring joy into the relationship.

GRID PLACEMENT

You can place a grid anywhere, but placing it with purpose can be especially helpful in creating the energy you need. For example, if you create a grid for sleep (amethyst in a ring of moonstone, for instance), it might be a good idea to place it in your bedroom or under your bed. Likewise, a grid for purpose may be good in a meditation area or your office. As I previously mentioned, I always have a learning grid in my classrooms when I teach. Some tips:

- Place it in the room where you think it is most relevant (see examples above). For example, if you've created a grid for healthier eating, the kitchen is a good choice, while if you created a grid to heal irritable bowel syndrome, it might go well in the bathroom.

- Place it in the center of your home and use clear quartz points to direct the energy outward.

- Use your fêng shui bagua and place it in the appropriate bagua areas.

The Crystal Alchemist

Grids and crystal combinations are fun because creating them gives you a chance to be an alchemist, combining colors, shapes, and energies to create a whole new vibe. When you intentionally combine crystals, it strengthens and transmutes the properties of the individual crystals and generates a more powerful and direct result that almost seems like magic. And this is just the start of bringing crystal alchemy into your life. You can also bring even more in by making it a part of your daily beauty routines.

CHAPTER 15

Crystal Personal Care

As crystals have grown in popularity in recent years, more brands have offered gemstone-infused personal care products, such as skin care lines, fragrances, and even makeup.

I love incorporating crystals into my self-care practices. Since I have been doing so, my skin has more of a glow, my hair is shiny and healthy, and I feel calm and balanced. Likewise, I really enjoy finding new ways to bring the energy of crystals into every aspect of my life.

So whether you're looking for facial care, makeup products, bath products, or something else, there are many ways to incorporate crystals into your daily self-care and beauty routines.

Gua Sha

Pronounced "gwasah," *gua sha* is a practice from traditional Chinese medicine in which the skin is scraped with a tool to draw blood to the surface. While this is typically a full-body treatment performed by a trained practitioner, it has been adapted to beauty practices as a form of facial treatment using a crystal gua sha scraping tool. You'll typically find these tools made from rose quartz or jade, although I've seen them occasionally made from other gemstones, as well. My gua sha tool is made from rose quartz.

Gua sha tools come in a few different shapes. They are thin and flat with rounded edges. A number of beauty brands offer gua sha tools. See "Resources" for a list of suppliers. You use the tool to lightly scrape the skin, which promotes lymph drainage and facilitates blood flow to the skin's surface, leaving it glowing.

Facial gua sha requires a light touch and lubricated skin. In full-body gua sha, the goal is for the practitioner to use enough force in the scraping to draw *petechiae*, which are small red or purple spots caused by microbleeds under the skin. Practitioners believe this allows oxygenated blood to flow to the scraped areas to bring about healing. In facial gua sha, petechiae aren't the goal, however, because nobody wants a bunch of red bumps on their face. Instead, you use the tool to scrape gently in an upward and outward direction. Using a facial serum helps keep the skin lubricated so the tool glides lightly over the skin, and the scraping also helps push the serum more deeply into the skin.

I perform facial gua sha every morning. It's a regular part of my beauty routine; it's the first thing I do every morning after brushing my teeth, and it takes less than five minutes. My skin glows throughout the day, and it's a great way to wake up.

To perform facial gua sha:

1. Wash your face with your preferred cleanser and pat it dry.

2. Apply toner to your face with a cotton ball or spritz it on and allow it to dry.

3. Choose a serum or facial oil to lightly lubricate your skin and neck. Spread it on the skin's surface in upward and outward strokes, but don't rub it in.

4. Now, starting at the base of your throat and working in an upward and outward direction, lightly scrape the edge of the gua sha tool along your skin's surface. I do one side of my neck and face at a time, starting at the back of my neck and scraping upward to the hairline, along one side of the neck scraping upward to the jawline, and then the front of my throat scraping upward to the base of my chin.

5. Continuing along the same side, begin lightly scraping your face with the tool, chin upward to lips, lips upward to nose, jaw upward along the side of the nose and cheek, along the nose, and along the eyes and forehead upward and outward to the hairline.

6. Lightly scrape underneath the eye and along the brow line in an outward direction toward and ending at the hairline.

7. Once you've scraped the entire side of your face, starting at your hairline at the top center of the forehead, scrape the edge of the tool following your hairline, down the side of your face, and down the side of your neck and jaw until you reach where your neck and shoulder connect. The goal here is to sweep any fluid that has accumulated in your upward scraping from the hairline down and out of your face region.

8. Repeat steps 4 through 7 on the other side of your face.

9. Apply your regular moisturizer.

10. Always wash your tool before storing it.

I've noticed I have fewer dark circles under my eyes, and the gua sha immediately eliminates any puffiness I wake up with. I like to keep my gua sha tool in the freezer after I wash it so it is cool and energizing.

Gemstone Facial Rollers

Another gemstone product that has seen increased popularity and availability in the marketplace is a gemstone facial roller. Like the gua sha tools, these are usually made from jade or rose quartz, although I've seen them in clear quartz and other gemstones as well. Most retailers that have gua sha tools also offer gemstone facial rollers (see "Resources").

The tool is a small, handheld roller with a gemstone handle. On either end is a gemstone cylinder that rolls as you run it along your face; it's like a personal massager for your face.

You can use a facial roller in conjunction with the gua sha or instead of it. I have two rollers, and I keep them both in my freezer. I like to use them once or twice a week as part of an entire crystal facial I do. Rolling a cool crystal across my face is energizing, and it helps promote fluid drainage, can be helpful for any swelling or discoloration associated with blemishes, and you can use it to roll serum or oils more deeply into your skin. They are also heaven to use when I have a headache. I roll them along the back of my neck and across my brow, jaw, and temples.

To use a facial roller:

1. Start with a clean, dry face.

2. Spritz your face with toner and allow it to dry.

3. Now, apply a facial oil or serum to your face, décolletage, and neck. Don't rub it in right away.

4. Starting at your chest, roll the roller in an upward direction, on your décolletage, neck, along your jawline, and over your entire face, always rolling in light strokes in an upward and outward direction.

5. Finish with your regular moisturizer.

6. Wash and dry your roller before you store it.

While it isn't necessary to keep the roller in the freezer or fridge, it's where I like to keep mine. On days when I have trouble waking up, I pull out the frozen facial roller, and it immediately puts some pep in my step and a glow in my skin.

Gemstone Beauty Products

You can find an array of types of gemstone-infused beauty products—in everything from cleansers to toners to facial masks, serums, eye creams, and moisturizers. Some products are infused with gemstones, meaning they use an infusion process similar to what I describe in the gemstone elixirs chapter to bring the gemstone's energy to the product. Others actually contain ground-up gemstones as part of their ingredient list.

These beauty products are for varying skin types, and they come at a variety of price points. Currently, I use gemstone-infused or gemstone-containing facial and body cleansers, toners, masks, serums, eye creams, and fragrances. See "Resources" for a list of some gemstone products.

Crystal Facials

I like to give myself a crystal facial at least once a week. This includes crystal rollers and gua sha, facial masks, and a crystal facial grid using rose quartz and aquamarine. It leaves my skin smooth, glowing, and healthy, and it helps me feel relaxed and peaceful. It's a great way to carve out some "me" time and bring more beneficial crystal energy into your life.

Here's my process for my crystal facial, which takes about 30 minutes.

1. Cleanse your skin with either a crystal exfoliating cleanser or use a crystal cleanser and an exfoliation brush to gently remove any dead surface skin.

2. Rinse thoroughly with cool water and pat your skin dry with a towel.

3. Apply a crystal-infused facial mask to correct any skin care issue you're working with, such as an exfoliating mask or a deep mineral mask.

4. Rinse the mask away with warm water and pat your skin dry.

5. Apply a crystal-infused toner with a cotton ball or spritz it on your skin.

6. Apply a crystal-infused serum or facial oil, but don't rub it completely into the skin.

7. Use a gua sha tool to perform gua sha as outlined earlier in the chapter.

8. Find a quiet space where you won't be disturbed. Lie comfortably on your back. Place two small aquamarines on your face—one on your third eye and one on your chin. On each cheek, place a rose quartz crystal. Close your eyes and relax for 10 to 15 minutes.

9. Remove the crystals. Apply a bit more of your facial serum and use the roller to roll it gently into the skin in an upward direction.

10. Apply a crystal-infused moisturizer and a crystal-infused eye cream.

More Ways to Incorporate Crystals into Your Beauty Routine

In addition to the many crystal facial care products, you can find just as many for bath, body, hair, and nails as well. I encourage you to experiment to find crystal bath and beauty products, including soaps, body lotions, shampoos, and more. You can even add homemade crystal elixirs to your bath or beauty products to fully pamper yourself with the energy of crystals. Doing this is a great way to bring even more crystal energy into your life. And when you're ready for more, you can also start to work with crystals using other healing practices.

CHAPTER 16

Using Crystals with Other Healing Practices

Healing doesn't exist in a vacuum. While you may be able to isolate a root cause of an issue, it's seldom as simple as finding a single cause, correcting it, and moving forward. That's because humans are more than just anatomy. We are body, mind, and spirit, and a host of complex factors contribute to every mental, emotional, physical, and spiritual condition. While health issues may seem as if they are simply bodily symptoms created by a single root cause, such as a case of lung cancer being caused by smoking, the truth is that everything we do, think, feel, experience, consume, breathe, and contemplate contributes to our overall health and well-being. While smoking may contribute to lung cancer, for instance, there are many other factors that likely do as well, including genetics, personal health habits, stress, beliefs, and multiple others. Disease, disharmony, imbalance, problems, or illnesses of any kind always arise as a result of multiple factors, life experiences, stressors, thoughts, beliefs, and patterns.

For example, it may seem easy to trace a common cold to an exposure to cold germs. But if exposure to cold germs were the only reason someone caught a cold, then how is it possible that two people can be exposed to the exact same germs, but only one gets sick and the other continues healthily on their way? We could say, of course, that one must have better immunity than the other, so the one with weaker immunity gets sick. But why? What contributed to that weaker or stronger immunity? Was it diet? Was it stress? Was it lifestyle habits, sleep, belief systems, genetics, constitution, or something else? Chances are, it is a combination of all these things that contributed to a simple, common cold that one person comes down with and the other avoids when both are exposed to the same germs.

And so it is with any issue, whether it is an illness, an unresolved emotion, a spiritual crisis, or something else. It's never simple to point to a single source that allowed that root cause to grow and fester and become disharmony. And due to this complexity in root causes, its often not as simple as finding a single "treatment" to remedy a situation. This is why I recommend taking a multifaceted approach to wellness: because just as there isn't a single "cause" for an issue, there's seldom a single "cure." While crystals offer a powerful way to shift and change energy in your life, combining them with other self-nurturing practices and healing modalities allows you a more comprehensive way to address the complex issues that make up the totality of human health and well-being.

Energy Tools and Self-Nurturing Practices

Here are some tools you can have in your arsenal that, when combined with crystals, can work synergistically to address the underlying causes of disharmonies that affect your well-being. While this isn't meant to be a comprehensive description of these activities, it is a great place to start as you continue to find ways to provide yourself opportunities for wellness.

MOVEMENT PRACTICES

Movement is a form of energy healing. When you move your body in any way, energy moves through all aspects of your physical and energy anatomy. So it is my belief that every movement practice is also an energy healing practice. However, some are gentler, kinder, and more in harmony with your being than others.

When I was in my late teens and early twenties, I wasn't always very easy on myself physically. I'm a member of the generation that came of age in the 1980s when the movement philosophy was "No pain, no gain." I believed in this wholeheartedly and pushed my body past its limit regularly.

I worked as an aerobics instructor, nutrition advisor, and personal trainer. I was a competitive bodybuilder who spent about three hours most days of the week in hard, punishing exercise. On top of this, I taught about 15 aerobics classes each week and ran several miles every day. In retrospect, it's probably not a surprise that one day my body screamed "enough!" and refused to allow such punishment any longer. The extent of my physical activity completely depleted my emotional, mental, physical, and spiritual energy. It was the start of my autoimmune disease, and my body refused to allow me to exercise like that anymore. I went from spending virtually all of my time in punishing physical activity to none. Not only that, but I was psychically exhausted as well. It took me months to restore the spiritual and emotional energy I'd depleted in my attempt to sculpt my body to perfection.

As a result of my experiences and the 20 years of illness that followed my punishing physical routine, I developed a much different philosophy of movement. I started to understand that movement could be about pleasure instead of pain, and that I could still be physically healthy while moving in ways that were pleasurable to my body instead of painful without depleting my energy stores.

And while there are still plenty of punishing physical activities you can use to whip your body into submission, I often recommend a gentler, more moderate approach. Fortunately, today there are many kind, gentle, pleasurable ways you can move that promote enjoyment and healing while still helping you stay fit and healthy. These include practice-based fitness activities such as yoga, tai chi, and Nia, all of which focus on gently moving energy through your body with an emphasis on the balance of body, mind, and spirit. Regardless of whether you choose gentle, intense, or a combination thereof, however, movement of any kind can become an energy practice if you engage in it with intention.

At first blush, it may seem that crystals are somewhat incompatible with movement practices. However, with some creativity, you can bring crystal energy into any fitness practice.

Visualize with a Crystal Before Moving

A brief, five-minute visualization before beginning any movement practice can help you set your intention for that session and can also help set the energy for the session. For example:

- Hold a garnet in your receiving hand and visualize it sending energy through your body before a high-energy movement session, such as running, hot yoga, or a high-energy martial art, like tae kwon do.

- Before a restorative yoga session or another form of gentle, healing movement, such as tai chi, hold a piece of rose quartz in your receiving hand and visualize it sending peace throughout your body.

- Before any session of activity that requires maximum blood flow, hold a piece of hematite or bloodstone in your receiving hand and visualize your red blood cells growing oxygenated and flowing freely throughout your body.

Use a Crystal to Ground You During or After a Session

Regardless of what type of exercise activity you engage in, after a session, you can wind up feeling ungrounded. It's one of the reasons why yoga sessions end with Shavasana, because lying on the floor in corpse pose helps bring your energy back into your body and ground you. You can also use crystals for this purpose after any type of movement practice. For example:

- Keep a grounding crystal, such as black tourmaline, in your workout bag and sit quietly for a few moments after your session holding the crystal in your receiving hand and visualizing sinking your energy into your body and out through the bottoms of your feet into the earth.

- Wear a piece of red hematite as a bracelet or keep one in your pocket throughout your session. If you start to feel ungrounded, close your eyes and focus on the grounding sensation of that crystal for a moment.

Place Crystals Around Your Movement Practice Space

If you engage in a movement practice at home, you can place crystals with intention around your workout space.

- Place carnelian in and around your movement practice space to enhance motivation.

- Place petrified wood in your movement space to increase stamina.

- Place green tourmaline in a movement space to increase strength and endurance.

- Place amethyst on the four corners of your yoga mat to increase focus and enhance communication with the higher self.

Program a Crystal with the Energy of Your Practice to Bring It with You Throughout the Day

You know how you feel when you finish a movement practice? You may feel bliss or peace. You may be more focused or notice more clarity. You may feel energized and euphoric. You may feel like you're ready to take on the world. As you go about your day, however, chances are these feelings fade as you're inundated with real life, and they don't return until your next movement practice session. Don't you wish you could bottle that feeling and take it with you so it's accessible, even outside of your movement practice? Programming a crystal makes this possible.

The idea is simple. At the end of your movement practice when you're in whatever wonderful mental, spiritual, physical, and emotional state you end up, hold a crystal in your giving, or dominant, hand, intend to transfer that energy to the crystal, visualize the energy transferring into the crystal, and then carry that crystal with you throughout the day. You can do this at the end of every movement session.

Clear quartz is ideal for this because it takes on the energy of intention easily and it amplifies energy as it stores it. Start with a piece of freshly cleansed clear quartz and pull it out of your gear bag immediately after your workout while you're still in your altered state.

SOUND HEALING

I have been a musician for more than 40 years, and sound is an important part of my personal energy healing practices. I teach and work as a sound healer, working with bronze Tibetan instruments—such as singing bowls and bells—crystal singing bowls, tuning forks, shamanic drumming, vocalizations, solfeggio, chanting and mantras, and music. For example, I mentioned using crystals with bija seed mantras to help balance the chakras in the meditation chapter.

Sound is vibration and, like crystals, it works through the process of entrainment to help balance and shift energy. All sound affects energy in different ways. You can see this in the work of Masaru Emoto, who, in his book *Hidden Messages in Water*, showed how various types of music, such as heavy metal, hymns, Gregorian chants, and classical music, significantly changed the crystalline structure of water that was frozen after it was exposed to various types of music. The results are astounding, with lovely and peaceful forms of music showing organized, beautiful crystalline patterns and loud, harsh music creating muddy or disorganized cell structure.

Sound is so evocative and powerful that it can leave you feeling peaceful, energized, focused, distracted, joyful, sad, or any other stop on the spectrum of human emotion. Combining the right sounds with the right crystals can double the effects, causing powerful energetic shifts that are even more significant than if you used either sound or crystals alone.

Use Crystals with Solfeggio Frequencies

Solfeggio frequencies are part of a six-tone scale used in Gregorian chants and other types of music. These frequencies are believed to create balance and healing. You can find solfeggio frequencies on YouTube, and there are many device apps that offer them, as well. Each frequency is associated with various physical, spiritual, mental, or emotional health issues. Typically, you listen to them through headphones with your eyes closed in a meditative state and allow them to shift your frequency. You can also combine them with crystals that harmonize with the solfeggio frequencies to increase their power. To do this, hold the corresponding crystal in your receiving, or nondominant, hand and focus on its energy as you listen to the solfeggio frequency.

- 396 Hz is associated with the color red and the root chakra. It liberates guilt and fear and can increase feelings of safety and security or disperse the ego's need for these things. Red crystals are best here, such as red hematite, spinel, or garnet.

- 417 Hz is associated with the color orange and the sacral chakra. The frequency can help create change, undo unhealthy patterns, and resolve discordant energy patterns. Hold carnelian while you meditate on this frequency.

- 528 Hz is associated with the color gold or yellow and the solar plexus chakra. The frequency facilitates transformation. Pyrite is a powerful crystal to use with this solfeggio frequency.

- 639 Hz is associated with the color green and the heart chakra. It facilitates the process of connecting with others and can help strengthen relationships and love. Green tourmaline and emerald are both excellent crystals to hold when listening to this frequency.

- 741 Hz is associated with the throat chakra and the color blue. Not surprisingly, this solfeggio frequency strengthens communication and listening and helps you express ideas and find solutions to long-term issues. Hold sodalite, lapis lazuli, or aquamarine when working with this frequency.

- 852 Hz is associated with the third eye chakra and the color violet or indigo. It facilitates higher guidance and a connection with your higher self. Charoite, amethyst, and sugilite are all good crystals to use with this frequency.

Chant Vowel Sounds to Align Chakras

Close your eyes, take a deep breath, and make a long, drawn-out vocalization of the vowel "a." Say, "aaaaa" (long a). As you do, notice where it vibrates in your body. Chances are, you feel it in your forehead and sinuses around your third eye. Just as this vowel sound activates and vibrates the third eye chakra, each chakra has an associated vowel sound that activates and balances it. Using crystals can facilitate this process.

Using the sounds and crystals identified in the table below, lie on your back and place a freshly cleansed crystal on each of your chakras. Then, chant each vowel sound, focusing on that chakra as you do. Feel the crystals and the sounds align, balancing each chakra. Hold each vocalization for as long as you can, chanting it three times each before moving on to the next. You can move upward through the chakras, from root to crown, if you need to energize or from crown to root if you need to ground.

Chakra	Sound	Crystal
root	"uh"	black tourmaline or hematite
sacral	"ooooo"	carnelian or sunstone
solar plexus	"oh"	citrine or yellow tigers eye
heart	"ah"	green tourmaline or malachite
throat	"eye"	blue lace agate or celestite
third eye	"aye" (long a)	amethyst or iolite
crown	"eee"	clear quartz or selenite

Take a Sound Bath with Crystals

Sound baths are a form of sound meditation where you lie back, close your eyes, and let the tones wash over you. They typically involve Tibetan or crystal singing bowls (or both), wind chimes, gongs, and other instruments that put you in a peaceful, relaxed, and often altered state. As a sound practitioner, I perform sound baths for others. You can often find people who perform these in local yoga studios. If you have sound healing instruments of your own, you can also create your own sound bath. They are also available from smartphone apps and on YouTube.

To take a sound bath (if you aren't the one playing the instruments), find a place where you won't be disturbed. Dim the lights, find a comfortable place to lie down (such as a yoga mat or some pillows), place crystals on or around you, lie back, and allow the sound to wash over you. Focus on the sounds and the energy of the crystals. If your focus shifts, return it gently to the sound and the crystals again.

To create a simple sound bath grid:

- Place a grounding crystal, such as a piece of red hematite, just below your feet.

- Place a very high-vibration crystal, such as phenacite or danburite, just above your crown chakra.

- In your dominant, or giving, hand, hold a piece of pink rose quartz or morganite.

- In your nondominant, or receiving, hand, hold a piece of celestite.

Drum with Crystals

Drumming is an active way of using sound to move into an altered state. Drumming can help release blocked energy, and many shamans use it as a way to journey into other realms. You can use any type of drum, such as a Djembe, bongos, or an indigenous hand drum. Use your hand or a drumstick to create a rhythmic pattern. Common drumming patterns include a heartbeat-type pattern (ba-BUMP) or a simple four-count pattern with an accent on one (BUMP bump bump bump, BUMP bump bump bump). As you drum, focus on your breathing, maintaining rhythm and the sounds you make. If your attention drifts, bring it gently back to your drumming.

Do this inside a ring of crystals, such as clear quartz, to amplify the energy. You can also place crystals around you in the four directions to signify the elements and increase the power of the drumming.

- North is the direction of the element water. Place a piece of aquamarine or iolite to the north to activate this element.

- East is the direction of the element air. Place a piece of moonstone or blue calcite to the east to activate this element.

- South is the direction of the element fire. Place a piece of carnelian or garnet to the south to activate this element.

- West is the direction of earth. Place a piece of onyx or jasper to the west to activate this element.

AROMATHERAPY WITH CRYSTALS

The growing popularity of crystal-infused aromatherapy products on the market is a testament to how well aromatherapy and crystals go together. In fact, the two seem made for each other. Just as crystals vibrate with the energy of the universe, so do plants. Aromatherapy oils, or essential oils, are distilled from the pure essence of plants, and they carry the vibration of the plants with them, infusing a space with the living essence and frequency of the plants. As with all other forms of energy healing, entrainment allows your energy to lock into phase with the energy of the essential oils to create a shift.

Aromatherapy lends itself to many uses, especially in conjunction with crystals. A few of my favorites follow.

Diffuse Essential Oils During Crystal Meditation

Diffusers send tiny droplets of essential oils into the air with water, allowing the fragrance to permeate the room. Let's look to our six areas for great essential oil, crystal, and meditation combinations.

Health and wellness. Strengthen general health by creating a turquoise crystal elixir and placing it in a diffuser with two drops of orange essential oil and one drop of cinnamon essential oil. Hold a piece of turquoise in your receiving, or nondominant, hand as you meditate on the mantra, "I am healthy."

Prosperity and abundance. Create a crystal elixir from citrine. Add it to a diffuser with four drops of bergamot essential oil and two drops of sandalwood essential oil. Hold the citrine in your receiving, or nondominant, hand. Close your eyes and visualize yourself living a prosperity-filled life.

Self-love and self-esteem. Create a crystal elixir from tigers eye. Add it to a diffuser with six drops of lemon essential oil. Hold the tigers eye in your receiving hand, close your eyes, and focus on your breathing, drawing your attention back to your breath if it wanders.

Forgiveness. Create a crystal elixir with peridot. Add it to a diffuser with four drops of sandalwood essential oil and four drops of lavender essential oil. Hold the peridot in your giving, or dominant, hand. Close your eyes and visualize the person you wish to forgive. Visualize them surrounded in light and repeat the mantra, "I forgive you. I release you."

Purpose. Create a crystal elixir with amethyst. Add it to a diffuser with four drops of frankincense essential oil and two drops of rosewood essential oil. Hold the amethyst in your receiving hand. Set the intention to receive information about your higher purpose by saying something such as, "Show me what I need to know about my purpose." Close your eyes, focus your attention on your third eye chakra, and breathe quietly. Watch the images that arise without judgment.

Love and relationships. Create a crystal elixir from rose quartz. Add it to the diffuser with three drops of jasmine essential oil. Hold a rose quartz in your receiving, or nondominant, hand, close your eyes, and visualize love flowing through the rose quartz, into your hand, and filling your entire being.

USE AROMATHERAPY MASSAGE AND CRYSTALS TO BALANCE CHAKRAS

Aromatherapy massage is an excellent way to balance your chakras, and combining it with crystals helps you achieve this even more easily. To do so, add one drop of the essential oils listed below to one teaspoon of a carrier oil, such as almond oil or jojoba oil, and massage it into each chakra in a counterclockwise motion, visualizing the massage activating that chakra. Then, lie back with each of the crystals listed below on each chakra and visualize the energy flowing through each chakra. Never use undiluted essential oils directly on the skin; always mix them with a carrier oil first.

Chakra	Essential Oil	Crystal
root	patchouli	hematite
sacral	orange	sunstone
solar plexus	lemon	citrine
heart	rose or rose otto	rose quartz
throat	blue chamomile	blue lace agate
third eye	lavender	amethyst
crown	sandalwood	clear quartz

Hands-On Energy Healing Modalities

There are numerous hands-on energy healing modalities you can seek or learn, such as Reiki, Quantum Touch, Healing Touch, Chios Energy Healing, Polarity Therapy, and Matrix Energetics. Each requires specialized training or attunement, and in order to experience these therapies, you need to seek someone qualified to offer them.

These hands-on energy healing modalities can be a powerful catalyst for energetic change. I am a Reiki master-teacher and find it to be a powerful form of hands-on energy healing that can release energetic blockages, correct imbalances, and allow the body, mind, and spirit to find a place of harmony and balance. While I'm not suggesting you learn to do these forms of energy healing yourself—unless you feel drawn to do so, of course—I am suggesting they may be helpful on your journey. If you have the opportunity to seek Reiki or another form of hands-on energy healing, I recommend you allow the experience at least once just to see what it's all about.

I use crystals in conjunction with my hands-on energy healing practices, and many practitioners I know who do various forms of energy healing use them as well. Crystals increase the power of the experience and can help it be more effective.

The other use for crystals in hands-on therapy is to bring the energy of the session home with you. There are two ways to do this.

HAVE THE PRACTITIONER PROGRAM A CRYSTAL FOR YOU

Bring a freshly cleansed clear quartz crystal with you to your session. At the end of the session, ask the practitioner if they would infuse the energy they used in the session into the crystal. Many are happy to do this, and it typically only takes a few extra moments for them to hold the crystal in their hands and infuse it with the energy. Then, you can carry that crystal with you or wear it and hold it in your receiving hand any time you wish to reinforce the energy of the session. The energy should hold for several days before it needs to be recharged.

INFUSE IT WITH YOUR ENERGY AFTER THE SESSION

You can also infuse a clear quartz crystal with your energy immediately after the session or during the session. To do this, at the close of the session or during the session, hold the clear quartz crystal in your giving, or dominant, hand. Intend for the energy of how you are feeling to transfer through you and into the crystal. Then, carry the crystal with you and hold it in your receiving hand when you want to recharge with the energy of that session. The energy should last for several days before it needs to be recharged.

Enhancing Your Energy

I've touched on a few of the many ways you can use crystals with other energy healing practices and modalities to bring even more crystal energy into your life. Crystals can strengthen your intentional activities to help bring and maintain energetic balance and harmony and maximize your efforts. It's another way you can use these powerful tools in your life to actively and passively shift energy.

All the methods I've covered in this section of the book are tools in your arsenal. You can pick and choose those that resonate for you or make up your own rituals based on what you intuitively feel is right for you.

You now have a solid foundation along with some good ideas about what energy you'd like to bring into your life and how to find and use crystals to facilitate that. You may even be feeling inspired to come up with your own uses, combinations, and rituals to create energetic shifts in your life.

There's one more piece of the puzzle that's essential if you want to create lasting energetic change: using your intention and directing your focus to create lifelong practices and habits that grow and evolve as your needs shift and change.

PART 4

THE CRYSTAL
HABIT

CHAPTER 17

Setting an Intention

Life is seldom stagnant, and everyone is always growing and changing. If you're working with crystals, this may be especially true for you right now because crystals facilitate change. As you move through your life, you have various needs at different times, and these needs and priorities are always shifting, as are the crystals you need to use to facilitate your ongoing growth. It's been my experience that whenever I create one desired shift, it opens my eyes to another, and then another, and then another. We are never "done." As long as we are embodied, we can continue to adapt, change, grow, and improve as we move through the stages and cycles of life.

So we must remain nimble. We must be willing to look at where we are, evaluate where we are going, and continuously adapt to meet new needs. And while it may seem that the need and desire to continuously grow, adapt, and change could feel as if we can never be satisfied with what we have, that isn't the case at all. It's perfectly possible to be vibrantly happy where we are while still seeking growth and change. Without that continued desired to grow, we stagnate. And in stagnation, we often grow complacent and become bored. Then our vibrant happiness slowly drains away because we are no longer challenging ourselves to become better versions of who we are.

Enter Intention

Intention allows us to manage our growth, and it can help us remain adroit as our needs and priorities shift. Combining intention with crystals helps us do just that. It is, in my humble opinion, our most powerful tool in creating satisfying lives full of compassion, kindness, prosperity, love, well-being, and purpose. Many people equate intention with goals, but I think they are different. A *goal* is something you *want* to do, have, or achieve. An *intention* an energy you *choose* to cultivate.

Here are a few examples:

- A goal is to become president of your company. The intention is to follow a sense of purpose to embody leadership and vision.

- A goal is to lose weight. The intention is to embody mental, physical, emotional, and spiritual health.

- A goal is to graduate with a PhD. An intention is to embody wisdom, knowledge, and understanding in order to serve your highest purpose.

In other words, your goals are what you want to do. Your intentions are what you choose to be. One is about what you do. The other is about who you are. Using crystals can support both. Intention exists to serve the highest and greatest good, not only for our embodied selves, but for our journey as spirits as well, and crystals combined with intentions make your intention even clearer and more powerful.

The Power of Intention

Intention is everything. Intention is the first, strongest, most important, and most powerful tool we have to create the lives we wish to live. Intention is our spiritual lodestar. It is our mission statement, our guiding purpose, the basis for our ethics and values, and the driving force behind almost every goal we set, thought we think, word we speak, and action we take. Intention is, at its very core, the basis of who we are.

Even if you haven't actively considered your intention or determined what it is, it exists inside of you, driving your choices. The problem is when we aren't aware of our intentions or haven't consciously considered and chosen them, we act unconsciously and often bring about unintended outcomes.

So in order to bring about conscious shifts and to create our lives intentionally, we need to give thought to what we truly desire; consider what our core ethics, beliefs, and values are; think about what truly serves our highest and greatest good; and choose who we wish to be and how we wish to make that manifest in our life. That is the basis of intention, and working with crystals can help us find what our true intention is and keep it at the forefront as we move through our ever-changing lives and priorities.

Some people are born knowing their intention and have a good focus on it throughout their life. However, for most of us, it's something we have to actively seek, consistently monitor, and repeatedly discover. As we grow and have different experiences in our life, we often come to understand things differently, and our intentions change. Sometimes intentions change, and we don't recognize they have until several days, weeks, months, or years down the line when we finally notice something seems "off." Other times, we consciously change our intentions and then wait for our personal habits to catch up. Intention can be capricious unless we consciously attempt to stay attuned to our own sense of divine guidance to tell us when our priorities need to shift and, along with them, our behaviors and choices.

Your Divine Guidance System

Everyone has a divine guidance system. Some people call it their gut or their intuition. It speaks to us in feelings, emotions, and dreams, and its language is simple. If we feel bad or uncomfortable, we are not following our divine guidance. If we feel good, we are. When our intentions are clear and serving our highest purpose, we feel a sense of "rightness," experience a mental click, or are able to remain in a positive and balanced emotional state. We feel like we're "in the groove," and our life flows easily and happily. When our intentions are unconscious, poorly defined, or don't serve our highest and greatest good, then we experience some kind of discomfort or disharmony, either in the activities we engage in, the thoughts we think, or the emotions we experience. Crystals can amplify divine guidance and keep us focused on what our intentions are.

The issue isn't that our divine guidance fails to offer insights. It's that we fail to listen. In fact, sometimes divine guidance speaks to us more loudly if we haven't listened, often in an explosive act I call the "universal two-by-four" that happens when we've failed to heed divine guidance so it smacks us upside the head. I've been smacked by the universal two-by-four more than once.

Several years ago, I was working for a company as a marketing communication specialist. It was tedious, boring work that I felt didn't contribute at all to society as a whole. The company's ethics didn't match my personal ethics, my immediate boss had a clear problem with women, and the corporate culture was one of fear. However, I was comfortable. They liked my work, paid me well, and allowed me several perks, including working from home four days a week. So for me, it was easier to stay than to leave in spite of my growing discomfort with everything the company did and stood for.

I wasn't happy in that job almost from the start. I didn't enjoy the work, and I always left after my one day a week at the office feeling downtrodden from dealing with my misogynist boss. Still, I ignored my growing discomfort because it was easier to stay than to go. And then, one day came the universal two-by-four. My boss wanted me to come into the office every day, and I lived three hours away. Because I couldn't meet that requirement, the company let me go after nine years. The universe had spoken, and though I felt I should be terrified and devastated, I was elated.

Unfortunately, because I didn't leave on my own terms, it took me several years to regain my financial footing, and those years were often a struggle financially. However, in the end, I wound up in a much happier place, working in what I believe is my life's purpose. If the universe hadn't smacked me with a two-by-four, I wouldn't be writing books, teaching classes, or doing all of these other activities that bring me joy. Fortunately, the universe knew my intention even when I was unwilling to recognize it myself, and it allowed me to eventually move on to serve my life's true purpose. I know that for now, my intention matches my highest and greatest good because I feel like I'm in the flow. My emotions are positive, I experience harmony in my health and relationships, and I have an inner comfort and ease. The moment I feel that ease slipping, I know I need to reexamine my intentions to determine whether it's time to shift them.

Using Crystals to Access Your Divine Guidance System

You can use crystals to access your divine guidance system, which can help you arrive at your true intention. I find this works especially well when seeking clarity through meditation or dreams. In order to keep my divine guidance activated and my intention at the forefront of my mind, I keep an amethyst crystal cluster on my bedside table, and every night before I go to sleep, I say to the universe, "Tell me what I need to know." Then, I sleep on it. I find I often wake in the morning with a strong, clear sense of purpose, an idea, an insight, or a dream I'm able to interpret to understand what the universe wants me to know.

I recommend doing this every night to help you focus on your intention. You can place an amethyst on your bedside table, under your pillow, or under the head of your bed to help keep these messages coming. Keep a notebook or recorder next to the bed because often these feelings or dreams are ephemeral and drift away as soon as you shift your focus to your day unless you write them down.

You can also seek divine guidance in meditation in the same way. I find moonstone is an excellent crystal for this, or you can use an amethyst. Lie back, place the stone on your third eye, say, "Tell me what I need to know," and then close your eyes and focus on your third eye. Pay attention to any messages that arise, and write them down when you emerge from your meditation.

Using Crystals to Maintain Focus on Your Intention

Once you are aware of your intention, keeping it in focus can help you act in a way that is consistent with your highest vision for yourself. And although you always need to be willing to shift intention as you grow and change, while you are in the flow, it's important to maintain focus and keep intention at the forefront as you move through your day.

RECORD KEEPER CRYSTALS

Record keeper crystals are particularly powerful for helping you maintain focus on your intention. They aren't a specific type of crystal, but rather a feature certain crystals have. A record keeper on a crystal is one that has a naturally occurring triangle-shaped etching on the faces of a crystal. You typically see them in quartz crystals, like clear or smoky quartz or citrine, but they are found on other crystals as well.

Record keeper crystals do two things: they hold a record of what your purpose is as a soul, even if you aren't yet aware of it, and they also can hold your current intention and help you determine whether it serves your highest and greatest good.

To use a record keeper crystal for either purpose, hold it in your receiving, or nondominant, hand as you focus on your third eye and say, "Tell me what I need to know," or gaze at the record keeper triangles while clearing your mind. Pay attention to the feelings and messages that arise, as the record keeper will help you understand whether you are meeting your highest purpose with your intentions. You can carry a record keeper crystal with you in a pocket to help you maintain focus on your intentions as you go through your day.

Using Crystals to Keep Things from Interfering with Intention

There are several things that can interfere with or detract from your focus on your intention. Below are some of the issues and crystals that can help you overcome them.

GETTING CAUGHT UP IN EGO

Ego is of the mind and body, not the spirit. And while a little ego is good in that it helps us maintain a sense of self, an out-of-control ego can lead to judgment, anger, criticism, lack of humility, self-sabotage, self-indulgence, and negative habits. The ego is a powerful force, and most of us spend our entire life trying to break free from its tyranny.

An excellent stone for ego is ametrine, which is a combination of citrine and amethyst. Ametrine connects the solar plexus chakra, which is the center of ego, to the third eye chakra, which is the center of divine guidance. To use ametrine for ego, lie on your back with a piece of ametrine on your solar plexus and a piece on your third eye. Visualize the energy flowing between these two chakras in a balanced fashion.

IGNORING YOUR DIVINE GUIDANCE SYSTEM

Nothing can force you to pay attention to your divine guidance system, not even the universal two-by-four. You have free will, and the universe takes that stuff seriously. So you can continue to choose to ignore divine guidance for your entire life if you wish. Chances are, divine guidance will get louder and louder, but it's always your choice as to whether you actually pay attention.

While nothing can make you pay attention to divine guidance, there are crystals you can use to help you hear what it is saying. As I previously mentioned, amethyst is probably the best to use for this, both in meditation and in dream work.

STRESSFUL LIFE EXPERIENCES

Sometimes life knocks us for a loop for a while, and we focus on matters at hand instead of paying attention to our spiritual growth and development. This is a natural reaction. For instance, when my dad was diagnosed with cancer a few months ago and wound up in hospice, for the period of his illness and several weeks after his death, that was where my focus was. I was focused first on my fear of losing my dad and then on my grief.

Stressful events, such as the death of loved ones, conflict at work, relationship issues, or poor health, often draw us into our feelings, and we lose sight of our plan and intentions. Sometimes some of these issues arise because we had already lost sight of our focus, but sometimes things are truly beyond our control, and we need to deal with what's immediately pressing before we can refocus on intention, which, incidentally, often changes in the wake of such experiences.

In the case of my dad's death, I had to focus on my grief. It was the healthy thing to do, and at first I tried to stuff it and ignore it by throwing myself into work. It quickly became apparent that wasn't getting me anywhere, so I worked on processing my immediate emotion so I could regain my footing and move forward.

One of the best crystals for these unexpected experiences that rock our worlds is Apache tears, a round form of obsidian that helps you release and equalize emotions. I carry Apache tears with me always to give to people who are going through catastrophic change, and I was grateful I had them as I processed my father's illness and death. Keep Apache tears with you at all times and cleanse them daily when you're going through intense emotional upheaval. You can even sleep with them under your pillow.

It's important during these times to allow yourself to experience the emotion fully so it passes through you and doesn't get stuck in you. Allow yourself to feel, and as the emotion inevitably passes and shifts, you can return to your focus on your intention.

HAVING A POORLY DEFINED SENSE OF SELF

Knowing who you are is different from being caught up in ego. Having a poorly defined sense of self means lacking understanding of your place in your life or in the universe. Like an overactive ego, however, a poor sense of self is a solar plexus chakra issue. It usually arises from underactive third chakra energy, while being driven by ego is the result of overactive third chakra energy. If you have a poor sense of self, you may have poorly defined boundaries, you may be unaware of your own true intentions, or you may be making someone else's intentions your own. Strengthening the energy of the solar plexus chakra can help.

As I discussed in earlier chapters, if your solar plexus chakra is underactive, a clear, yellow crystal can help amplify its energy so you can develop a stronger sense of self. I recommend citrine for this. Wearing a citrine pendant on a long chain can help strengthen your sense of self and amplify your third chakra energy. Cleanse it daily.

NOT SPEAKING OR LIVING YOUR TRUTH

If you aren't rooted in your own truth, or if you are unwilling to speak or live your truth, then it will be difficult to maintain focus on your true intentions. Speaking and living your truth is connected to two chakras, your sacral chakra, where your integrity forms, and your throat chakra, which is related to speaking your truth.

Sunstone in iolite, which are two crystals that often form together, is the perfect remedy for imbalance in these two chakras. If you can't find sunstone in iolite, then you can also use each crystal separately. Meditate holding each of these crystals. If you have one that has both sunstone and iolite, hold it in your receiving, or nondominant, hand as you meditate. If you have one of each stone, then hold the iolite in your giving hand and the sunstone in your receiving hand. As you meditate, repeat the mantra, "I live my truth, I speak my truth."

ENGAGING IN PATTERNS OF NEGATIVE THINKING

It's easy to get caught up in negativity, but maintaining focus on negative thought patterns can detract from your focus on your intention. If you spend a lot of time thinking negatively or you spend a lot of time around someone who does, I recommend wearing a hematite ring on your receiving hand if you're around someone who speaks negatively, or on your giving hand if you engage in negative thought patterns. The ring will absorb negativity. When it breaks, return it to the earth and get a new one. Cleanse the ring daily.

What to Do If Your Intention Changes

As I mentioned earlier, intention changes throughout your life, and that's nothing to worry about. In fact, I'd be more likely to worry if my intention didn't change than if it did. As you grow and learn, you reach for something new. It's a constant process of reinvention that allows you to continue to grow and expand as a spiritual being.

So if your intention changes, don't worry. There's nothing you need to do other than focus on your new intention, test it with your divine guidance system, and see if the new one suits you well. Then, allow for change, be ready to adapt, and always check in to ensure you are continuing to meet your soul's highest purpose. And once you have your intention firmly in sight, you can maintain focus by creating mantras or affirmations.

CHAPTER 18

Making a Mantra or an Affirmation

I believe in the power of mantras and affirmations. About 20 years ago, I was in an unhappy place in my life. My marriage was unhealthy, and so was my body. I was broke. I hated my job. So I decided to write affirmations. First, I visualized what I truly wanted my life to be, and then I formed a series of positive statements about those desires. Every night, I wrote those affirmations five times each in a notebook. I did it for months.

Life intervened, and I eventually stopped writing my affirmations. Fast-forward several years. I was remarried. I had a new career. I was in the process of moving into a new home when I came across one of my old notebooks. I opened it and saw it was filled with the affirmations I'd written all those years before and discovered that in them, I'd described exactly the life I was now living.

What Are Affirmations and Mantras?

Mantras and affirmations are positive statements you use to reinforce your intentions. In general, mantras tend to be one- or two-word statements of intention, such as "peace," while affirmations are fully formed sentences such as, "I am peaceful." In this chapter, I'm going to use the terms interchangeably. You can speak them aloud, write them, type them, or repeat them silently in meditation. When you combine them with crystals, you strengthen their power to bring about change.

In the meditation chapters, I talked quite a bit about using mantras and affirmations in meditation practices, but I want to offer you some guidelines for creating your own effective affirmations and using crystals to enhance them.

Guidelines for Affirmations

Affirmations should always be created as a positive statement of what you wish to manifest in your life. They should always start with "I," followed by a statement of your intention as if you already have what you are affirming. For example, if you want to lose weight, the affirmation might be, "I am vibrantly healthy, and I maintain a healthy weight," while a mantra might be, "Health." If the affirmation is to change your eating habits, then you might say, "I eat foods that are nutritious and support my vibrant good health," while a mantra might be, "Nourished."

Avoid making statements as negatives in affirmations or statements of want. So instead of saying, "I am not fat," you would say, "I maintain a healthy weight." And instead of saying, "I want lots of money," say, "I give thanks that I am prosperous."

Crystals and Affirmations or Mantras

With these simple guidelines in mind, let's look at some affirmations and mantras you can create for each of the six most common areas of interest and how you can use crystals to strengthen an affirmation's intention.

HEALTH AND WELLNESS

As I've mentioned frequently, the crystals you use to support health and wellness will depend on what health issues you are dealing with. Match the chakra to the health issue and choose a crystal for that chakra. Turquoise is a good crystal for strengthening health overall.

You can use any of the following affirmations for health while holding the appropriate crystal in your receiving hand or lying with the crystal on the corresponding chakra. Mantras for health:

- Health

- Vibrant health

- Good health

- Wellness

- Well-being

Affirmations for health:

- I am grateful I am vibrantly healthy.

- Every cell of my body vibrates with the energy of good health.

- My body is strong and healthy.

- I engage in habits that nourish my body and support its good health.

PROSPERITY AND ABUNDANCE

Abundance issues originate in the second chakra. Although citrine is considered one of the strongest stones for abundance, second-chakra stones, such as carnelian or green stones, which are the color of money, are also good to hold in your receiving, or nondominant, hand while you affirm any of the following. Mantras for prosperity:

- Abundance

- Wealth

- Prosperity

Affirmations for prosperity:

- I give thanks to the universe that I am abundant.

- I am grateful for prosperity, which flows to me from all channels.

- I gratefully receive abundance from the universe.

- I have everything I need to live abundantly.

SELF-LOVE AND SELF-ESTEEM

Because self-esteem is a solar plexus chakra issue, yellow tigers eye is one of the most powerful stones you can use to boost yours. Pyrite also works well. Lie back, place the stone on your solar plexus chakra, and repeat any of the following mantras and affirmations. Mantras for self-esteem:

- Self-love

- I'm worthy

Affirmations for self-esteem:

- I approve of myself and love myself unconditionally.

- I know who I am, and I appreciate my strengths and good qualities.

- I am worthy of my own approval and respect.

PURPOSE

Affirmations about purpose focus on the purpose. State that purpose as if you already have it, offering gratitude. The stone you choose depends largely on what that purpose is. For example, if your purpose is to teach, you might choose a piece of blue calcite. If your purpose is maintaining your own sobriety or helping others maintain their sobriety, you might choose amethyst. Hold the stone in your giving, or dominant, hand as you affirm or use a mantra. Mantras for purpose:

- Purpose

- Soul's path

Affirmations for purpose:

- I am grateful I am serving my soul's highest purpose.

- Everything I think, do, and say serves my highest and greatest good.

- I am walking the path my spirit wishes me to in service of my highest purpose.

FORGIVENESS

As with love issues, forgiveness is a heart chakra issue. Therefore, a heart stone, like rose quartz or peridot, can help you release and forgive. Hold one stone in each hand or lay them on your heart chakra and visualize the person you wish to forgive as you repeat any of the following affirmations and mantras or make up your own. Mantras for forgiveness:

- Forgive

- Release

Affirmations for forgiveness:

- I forgive you and release you to a happy and fulfilled life.

- I release you with love and allow you to release me.

- I cut the ties of hurt and anger that hold us together and release us each to our highest good.

LOVE AND RELATIONSHIPS

With a focus on the heart chakra, green and pink crystals are ideal to hold in your receiving hand or lie with them on your heart chakra as you repeat your affirmations and mantras. Morganite is one of my favorites for this type of work. Mantras for love and relationships:

- Unconditional love

- Joyful love

- Community

Affirmations for love and relationships:

- I have a variety of loving and satisfying relationships and friendships in my life.

- I am grateful the universe has provided me with a loving partner.

- I give love freely, and it returns to me through friendships and relationships.

- My relationships are joyful and abundant.

Make Them Your Own

Whether you use some of the mantras and affirmations I've provided or make your own, when you use them with crystals, they become a powerful method to direct your intention. Whenever possible, try to create your own mantras and affirmations because when they come from you, they more closely suit your own needs and become stronger, more powerful statements to the universe of your true purpose. Then, once you have those mantras and affirmations ready, breathe life into them by creating habits and rituals that empower you to live your life's purpose.

CHAPTER 19

Making It a Habit

Your quiver is full. You have virtually every tool you need to harness the power of crystals to bring your intentions to life, harmonize and balance energies, and live each day with intention and purpose. Now all you need to do is choose to use them.

I have a confession to make. I'm a dabbler. Some might even call me a dilettante. I love learning new things. I consider myself a lifelong learner and devour knowledge with great enthusiasm. Some of it, such as energy healing and crystals, I master and incorporate enthusiastically into my life. With others, I intend to incorporate it into my life, but eventually I forget about it and drop it altogether. It's why I no longer make kombucha or paint canvases. While they were fun to learn and dabble in for a while, I failed to turn them into a regular part of my life regardless of how much I enjoyed them as I learned.

So what's the difference between kombucha and crystals? For me it's whether I turn it into a habit. For each new activity or concept I've learned, I originally had sufficient interest in it and enthusiasm for it to want to learn it in the first place. However, while I liked it all, I only did the work required to make some of it a habit.

How to Instill a Habit

Studies show it takes about 21 days of consistent repetition to create a new habit. If we miss a day, the 21 days starts all over again. If we don't restart the 21 days, then chances are we drop the activity or only engage in it intermittently when we don't have anything better going on.

I know this firsthand. I am a reformed serial killer of plants. My son coined the term "plant serial killer" for me because I was never able to keep my plants alive. This happened because I didn't make watering them a habit. Then, one day I decided I really wanted the energy of plants in my home for any number of reasons, and because it was important to me, I downloaded a watering app, made a habit of checking it daily, and on days I forgot, the app reminded me. I watered my plants according to the schedule my watering app reminded me of, and if I forgot to check my app on a given day, it sent me a push notification. My plants are still alive, and I check my watering app daily without needing push notifications any longer because I did this for 21 days in a row. My plants thank me.

MAKE IT A PRIORITY

If you don't see the value in doing something, then you will be far less likely to make it a habit. If you truly want to cultivate an energy in your life, such as the use of crystals, you need to learn enough to know why you might want to do so. So this, then, is the most important step in developing a habit: having sufficient desire to make it into one. It needs to matter to you. If it doesn't, then you're never going to do what it takes to make it a habit.

SET A REMINDER

Once something is important enough for it to become a habit, you need to establish a way to remember to do it every day. In the case of my perceived inability to meditate, I actually set reminders on my phone for the first several weeks. With the gua sha I do now, I made it the first thing I did in the morning after brushing my teeth so it wasn't easy to forget.

You can also use crystals as a reminder. For example, set a record keeper crystal in your line of sight and every time you look at it, perform some action related to whatever habit you're trying to establish. For instance, when you see your record keeper, pick up a crystal and repeat one of your affirmations. Taking these small steps every time you are reminded will help you establish a habit quickly.

CHOOSE ONE HABIT AT A TIME

Give your new habit the focus it deserves by creating only one habit at a time. Allow for that one to become firmly rooted before you move on to the next. So start small. Choose one crystal use or activity. Instill it as a habit, and then choose another.

BUILD ON EXISTING HABITS

You can also build a big habit by engaging in a series of smaller habits. For instance, start with your affirmation holding a crystal whenever you see your record keeper. Next, set aside five minutes to turn that into an affirmation or visualization session once or twice a day. By building to bigger habits starting with smaller habits, it psychologically seems more attainable and achievable.

GET RIGHT BACK ON THE HORSE

What happens if you miss a day with one of your new habits? Either do it as soon as you remember, or put it right back in your schedule the following day. After the initial 21 days, it isn't going to hurt you to miss a day here and there. Just make sure you return to your habit as soon as you possibly can. If you let it go too long, you'll need to start again. If after a few failed attempts, you just can't bring yourself to establish the habit, then you may want to reevaluate and decide if it's really that important to you.

The Value-Intention-Action Pipeline

Creating a habit follows the value-intention-action pipeline. First, you have to place enough value in the desired activity that you want to develop a habit. From that value arises your intention to continue to pursue the activity. From that intention arises the action you need to take to meet your original value or desired behavior. Each successive step occurred because the one leading to it was in place.

CHOOSE YOUR HABITS BASED ON PERSONAL VALUES

You've received a lot of information about using crystals in your life. It's up to you to decide what resonates with you and what doesn't. From this, you can determine what your personal values are. Which outcomes are you seeking that are most important to you? These are your personal values. From there, choose the practices that support them, one at a time.

USE CRYSTALS AS A PHYSICAL AND ENERGETIC REMINDER OF YOUR HABITS

You can use crystals to remember to use crystals. Place them in your environment or wear them, and when you notice them, engage in the activity you are trying to set as a habit. You can also reaffirm your intention each time you notice the crystal—it only takes a split second to do so.

The Crystal Habit

When I first incorporated crystals into my life, I started small. But as I established one habit, the crystals served as a reminder to create new habits. It became a practice that has grown into something that vastly enriches my life and helps me live deliberately and intentionally in service of my highest and greatest good. The crystals have created a feedback loop that spirals upward energetically, with one practice leading to another, allowing me to focus on creating a life of purpose and joy.

You Have the Tools to Change Your Experience

Once upon a time, there was a young woman who was living life in pain. She wasn't happy, and she often felt like she was just treading water, barely getting by. One day, a persistent health condition prompted her to go to a different kind of doctor. The good doctor placed a crystal on the young woman's throat, and a dam burst. It was the start of everything.

That is the beginning of my crystal story. It started 20 years ago. There have been fits and starts. There have been detours and side trips. There have been universal two-by-fours. There's been backsliding. But there has also been growth, joy, purpose, and so much more. It's my journey, and I wouldn't change a moment of it. A single crystal planted a seed that, with my attention and intention, has grown, flowered, and flourished into a big, beautiful, bold, purposeful life.

This is the start of your journey. This book caught your eye for a reason. Something in it called to something inside of you. It is your call to action. What will you do with it?

You have the tools to change your life. You've always had those tools, but perhaps you didn't know what to do with them or how to use them. Now you have some ideas. You possess inside of you the seeds necessary to make magic, and your life is fertile soil, waiting for you to plant them.

You don't have to plant every seed. Maybe only one or two appeal to you right now, so start there. Making magic doesn't have to be difficult or complicated. It starts small with a single habit here, a crystal there. Find just one that speaks to you. Engage with it in a way that feeds your soul. Allow the fire to slowly build. Feel your own power.

Crystals are the seeds. You are the soil. Plant one. Nurture it. Love it. And as you water it with your intention, magic can happen. You have everything you need. You have the tools to become a crystal alchemist.

Acknowledgments

A lot happened in my life while I was writing this book. In fact, more than usual happened. Through this, I came to understand how important certain people are in my life. So first and foremost, I need to thank those people who have propped me up and reminded me who I am and what is important during trying times, including my husband Jim; my sons Kevin and Tanner; my friends Kristen Gray, Kasci Lawrence, Nicole Strickland, Alli Richards, and Andy Skinner; my mom Brenda Riseland; and my sisters Julie Hoerner and Jenny Jim.

My journey in crystals, energy healing, and metaphysics has been one populated by wonderful people from whom I have learned so much. Michaela Rand and Ashley Barrett both inspired me on my crystal journey. I'm also grateful for the many teachers who have helped me over the years, from my Reiki master Howard Batie to my Nia "moms" Christina Mae Wolf and Laurie Bass. I'm also grateful to Tristan David Luciotti and Seth Michael for giving me a teaching home, and Cheryl Knight and Chad Wilson for giving me a writing home, as well as many of my fellow travelers, teachers, and students. I can't list them all because there are too darn many, but know that for all who have been part of my journey or allowed me to be part of yours, I am profoundly, deeply, passionately grateful.

Resources

Home Stores with Crystals

TJ Maxx

HomeGoods

Online Crystal Shops

Etsy (http://etsy.com)

eBay (http://ebay.com)

Healing Crystals (http://healingcrystals.com)

Crystal Subscription Crates

Cratejoy (http://cratejoy.com)

My Crystal Bliss (http://mycrystalbliss.com)

Tamed Wild (http://shoptamedwild.com)

Solfeggio Music

Glenn Harrold Solfeggio Smartphone Apps (http://glennharrold.com)

Solfeggio Sonic Meditation Bundle by Diviniti Publishing LTD

Jewelry

Tools for Evolution Crystal Jewelry (http://exquisitecrystals.com)

Gua Sha Tools and Gemstone Rollers

Sephora (http://sephora.com)

Ulta Beauty (http://ulta.com)

Herbivore Botanicals (http://herbivorebotanicals.com)

Aquarian Soul (http://shopaquariansoul.com)

Amazon (http://amazon.com)

Anthropologie (http://anthropologie.com)

Nordstrom (http://nordstrom.com)

Gemstone-Infused Beauty Products

Lotus Wei is a line of floral and gemstone fragrances, serums, and elixirs. My personal favorite is their Joy Juice fragrance line, which is infused with garnet. (http://lotuswei.com)

Aquarian Soul features botanicals, essential oils, and crystals in bath, body, and facial products. They also have a fantastic headache serum called Headache Magic that's infused with clear quartz and amethyst. (http://shopaquariansoul.com)

Pacifica offers a line of reasonably priced cruelty-free, vegan skin care solutions infused with crystals with delicious scents like watermelon and lemongrass. (http://pacificabeauty.com)

Själ Skincare is a high-end line of skin care products infused with and containing crystals and minerals. I love their Kashmir Saphir, which is a perfecting mask that contains ground-up sapphires. (http://sjalskincare.com)

Herbivore Botanicals uses crystals in many of their products, which are vegan, cruelty-free, ethically sourced, and all natural. (http://herbivorebotanicals.com)

La Prairie is a luxury line of skin care products, some that contain precious gemstones. (http://laprairie.com)

MineralFusion offers an array of crystal-containing beauty products. (http://mineralfusion.com)

Gemology Cosmetics adds crystals to their entire line of beauty products for women and men. (http://gemologycosmetics.com.au)

Karen Frazier is a metaphysical practitioner, intuitive energy healer, Reiki master teacher, and author of several books. She writes a monthly metaphysics and energy healing column for *Paranormal Underground* magazine, and writes articles on topics such as tarot, feng shui, and astrology for www.lovetoknow.com. Frazier is trained in multiple energy healing modalities; holds advanced degrees in metaphysics, including a master's and doctorate in the metaphysical sciences; and is writing a dissertation on how sound can affect healing. She teaches classes on Reiki, crystals, sound healing, energy anatomy, feng shui, and more in Portland, OR. Her books include *Crystals for Healing, Reiki Healing for Beginners,* and *Higher Vibes Toolbox.*

MORE BOOKS for the SPIRITUAL SEEKER

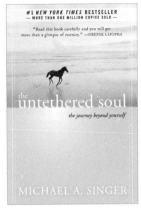
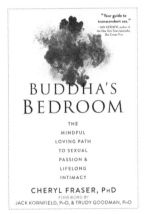

Register your **new harbinger** titles for additional benefits!

When you register your **new harbinger** title—purchased in any format, from any source—you get access to benefits like the following:

- Downloadable accessories like printable worksheets and extra content
- Instructional videos and audio files
- Information about updates, corrections, and new editions

Not every title has accessories, but we're adding new material all the time.

Access free accessories in 3 easy steps:

1. Sign in at NewHarbinger.com (or **register** to create an account).

2. Click on **register a book**. Search for your title and click the **register** button when it appears.

3. Click on the **book cover or title** to go to its details page. Click on **accessories** to view and access files.

That's all there is to it!

If you need help, visit:

NewHarbinger.com/accessories

new harbinger
CELEBRATING
40 YEARS